———— How to Live ————

A Guide to Everyday Budgeting and Self-sufficiency

Gill Govier

publishing

Copyright © 2009 by W & H Publishing. All rights reserved. No part of this work may be disclosed to any third party, translated, reproduced, copied or disseminated in any form or by any means except as defined in the contract or with the written permission of W & H Publishing.

First published in 2009 by
W & H Publishing
Apple Tree Cottage, Inlands Road, Nutbourne, PO18 8RJ

Text and Cover Design Wendy Craig
Cover Photograph Courtesy of istock
Printed and Bound in the UK by CPI Antony Rowe

Acknowledgements

I should like to thank all my friends and family for the support and encouragement given to me while researching for this book, and particularly the following friends who provided specialist knowledge and introduced me to new friends and neighbours who have already taken a key step towards self-sufficiency:

Caroline and Terry Alderton, Gill Bacon, Chris and Carme Boswell, Marian and Pete Bracey, Linda Cohen, Richard Cowell, Piers Cunningham, Munira Grainger, Rhoda Long, Briony and Reg Marjason, Gill and Ahmet Mehmet, Ruy and Paula Pinto, Emma Pitrakou, Lyn Powis.

British Library Cataloguing in Publication Data
A CIP record for this book is available from the British Library
ISBN 978-0-9561091-1-8

CONTENTS

Introduction   **5**
Everyday Budgeting 5
Self-sufficiency 6
How to Live on Less 6
Time to Break Even 7
The "Reality Check" Rating 8
Incremental Savings 9
Recipes 9

Chapter 1:
A Toolkit of Techniques for Living on Less   **11**
The Shopping Revolution 11
Strategy and Tactics 12
A Toolkit of Techniques for Living on Less 12
    Budgeting 13
    Planning 15
    Internet 16
    Credit vs Cash 20
    Shops and Outlets 22
    Timing 25
    Self-sufficiency 26

Chapter 2: Energy, Water and Fuel   **27**
Electricity 27
    Saving Money on Electricity 27
    Self-sufficiency: Generating Electricity 30
Heating 38
    Saving Money: Conserving Heat 38
    Self-sufficiency: Generating Heat 42
Lighting 45
Water 48
    Saving Money by Reducing Domestic Water Usage 48
    Self-sufficiency: Collecting Rainwater 51
Fuel 53
    Saving Money by Spending Less on Fuel 53
    Bio-mass 54

Chapter 3: Home and Leisure　　　　　　　　　　59
House and Home 59
Travel 61
Holidays 63
Days Out 64
Fitness 65
Smaller Items: Clothes, Books, Music 66
Computer and Communications 67
Incremental Income 68
Self-sufficiency Around the Home 70
    Natural Cleaning Products from your Store Cupboard 70
    Reduce – Reuse – Recycle 73
    Natural, Home-made Cosmetics 75
    Natural Pest Control (Indoors) 82
    Arts and Crafts 83

Chapter 4: Food, Drink and a Few Bits More　　　85
Saving Money on Everyday Consumables 86
    Shopping 86
    Cooking and Eating 88
    Stocking the Garden 90
Self-sufficiency 91
    The Productive Garden 92
    Natural Pest Control (Outdoors) 126
    Compost Contents 131
    Beverages 134
    Livestock 149
    Foraging 175

Index 187

INTRODUCTION

How to Live on Less is about taking a new and exciting look at financing our everyday life and the ways in which we can achieve the same, or similar, for less. Just because we want to economise doesn't mean resorting to penny-pinching or drastically reducing our quality of life in order to afford what we want. It's about understanding our spending patterns, learning new habits and taking advantage of a range of smarter, cheaper ways of sourcing, acquiring and using those products we need or desire.

Reducing expenditure and waste falls broadly into two main areas:

- Everyday Budgeting: setting and sticking to realistic, achievable targets, whether in energy or fuel consumption, spending capital or cash, feeding the family, etc.
- Self-sufficiency: the ability to produce some or all of what we use and consume

Several themes are used throughout the book to illustrate *How to Live on Less*:

- making simple economies, e.g. turning off lights, swapping to a cheaper insurance, using the car less or driving more efficiently
- finding a way to acquire the same for less, e.g. using a discount voucher, paying by direct debit, bartering goods and services
- developing new habits, e.g. cooking from scratch, using the Internet, developing a practical new craft or skill
- changing lifestyle, e.g. producing our own fruit and vegetables, raising livestock, ditching the car

Everyday Budgeting

The objective of this book is to provide a broad range of ideas to help you live on less. By this I mean achieving one, some or all of the following:

- spending less
- consuming/using less
- making what we already have go further
- reusing or recycling items
- potentially, finding incremental income just by using our skills and sweating our assets
- taking a step towards self-sufficiency (see later)

HOW TO LIVE ON LESS

You probably won't be able to achieve each of these ideas in every area of your life. For example, it would be difficult to "spend less" on your mortgage without causing a few alarm bells to ring with your lender! But you could have your home earn you extra income if you are prepared to rent out a spare room or possibly share your garden.

The aim throughout the book is to present a set of easy-to-use mechanisms which will help you reduce the final cost of what you want to acquire without compromising on quality. Not all techniques work for all scenarios, so I suggest you familiarise yourself with each of the tools identified in the toolkit to apply the most appropriate technique to each individual purchase.

Self-sufficiency

True self-sufficiency – the ability to supply all our energy needs, feed the family, keep ourselves clean and healthy and potentially derive income from products that we make ourselves – may well be beyond the capability, even interest, of many of us. The BBC sitcom of the 70s *"The Good Life"* portrayed one couple's attempts at such a life in a light-hearted way, but nevertheless also showed just how difficult and time-consuming (yet ultimately rewarding) it would be to achieve full self-sufficiency.

How to Live on Less presents some practical steps a town-based family can take towards a self-sufficient lifestyle. It does not necessarily involve turning your back garden into a pigsty – unless, of course, you have the space and the desire to rear pigs for bacon, pork or breeding, in which case turn to the Livestock section to get started. But it does involve considering small, incremental changes to the way we live, understanding how we use (and waste) energy, and what foodstuffs we could easily grow or forage for ourselves.

How to Live on Less

Each chapter is dedicated to a different theme; for example, Energy, Home and Leisure, Food and Drink. As I prepared the content of this book, I had a set of criteria in mind to determine whether it would be possible to live on less without substantially changing quality of life, or indeed to become self-sufficient, either fully or partly, in the supply of each commodity:

INTRODUCTION

- Am I taking advantage of all the modern tools and techniques of acquiring what I need – online shopping, discount vouchers, trading, timing?
- Is it possible to replace my current supply (of electricity, eggs, bath oil, etc.) with something of at least equal quality that I have produced myself? If yes, how much investment do I need to make of my time and money, and how long will it take to pay for itself?
- Would it be possible to derive any income from surplus produced as a result of my self-sufficiency efforts or from goods and services that I can provide?
- If I choose not to replace my current supply, for whatever reason, can I reduce what I currently purchase without significantly altering my quality of life so that I have more disposable income – thus instantly living on less or providing the funds to invest in one of the self-sufficiency projects?
- Finally, where replacement or reduction are not feasible or cost-effective options, is there the possibility to reuse or recycle resources to keep waste to a minimum and dispose of what I no longer want sensibly and sensitively?

Time to Break Even

I have attempted in several sections to give some guidance on how much a particular change of habit or self-sufficiency venture might cost, what savings can be made over current-day expenditure, and any income the activity could potentially generate. In doing so, I have introduced the concept of Time to Break Even.

The Time to Break Even is the amount of time it takes for the cost of an investment to be repaid through savings in bills or income from sale of products. Once the Time to Break Even has elapsed, all savings or income, are effectively profit.

As an example, I have provided a simple estimate in the Beekeeping section that one hive plus all its paraphernalia will probably cost around £300 up front. However, the hive should generate around 27 kg (60 lb) of honey each year, which we could arbitrarily divide between, say, 2 kg for your own use and 25 kg (i.e. fifty 500 g jars) to sell. Ignoring for the moment the effects of inflation, if you could then sell 500 g (just over 1 lb) at £3 per jar, you would generate (25 kg / 500 g) x £3 = £150 per year, making the Time to Break Even £300 / £150 = 2 years. After the two years, the £150 becomes pure profit.

Throughout this book, the Time to Break Even has been worked out purely as an example using current-day figures and assumptions – you will need to revise my calculations with up-to-date or personalised figures and possibly change the assumptions to fit changing circumstances in order to work out the actual break-even time for your particular investments.

The "Reality Check" Rating

I have also made an attempt to rate how easy/difficult, quick/time consuming, cheap/expensive the ideas presented might be. Reference will be made to the Reality Check as indicated by the following symbols. These will help you decide what initiatives you might try out according to how much time, effort and money you are prepared to invest, whether there is a positive impact on the environment, and the potential for additional income.

(Y)	No effort required	Very easy
Y	Small amount of effort or skill required	Reasonably easy
Y Y	Some effort or skill required	Practice makes perfect!
Y Y Y	Substantial effort or skill required	Difficult
(☉)	Takes no time	
☉	Takes a small amount of time	(Minutes/hours)
☉☉	Takes a fair amount of time	(Hours/days)
☉☉☉	Takes considerable amount of time	(Days/weeks)
(£-)	Little or no investment required	(Less than £10)
£-	Small investment required	(£10-£100)
££-	Some investment required	(£100-£1,000)
£££-	Significant investment required	(Over £1,000)
£+	Modest income possible	(Less than £100 pa)
££+	Some income possible	(£100-£1,000 pa)
£££+	Good income possible	(Over £1,000 pa)
♥	Good for the environment	

INTRODUCTION

Incremental Savings

Many of the savings indicated in this book may seem small, even insignificant, when judged entirely on their own. For example, the annual saving on your heating bill by changing to a condensing boiler from a standard boiler may be only about £100 (ignoring for the moment the capital cost of making such a change and the Time to Break Even); but when combined with other savings – changing to energy-efficient light bulbs, supplying your own fruit and vegetables, using loyalty cards and discount vouchers in a more focused manner – these savings start to add up and suddenly £100 a year becomes £500 a year simply by making small changes in your habits or taking more responsibility for providing what you eat.

Recipes

There are a number of recipes associated with individual chapters, some for food, others for beverages or home-made products (e.g. floor cleaner). Where food recipes are provided, these are to feed four people, unless otherwise specified.

chapter 1

A Toolkit of Techniques for Living on Less

Eating less ready-made food, consuming fewer kilowatt-hours of energy, reusing what we already have and becoming more self-sufficient in providing for our needs are all excellent methods for living on less, and throughout this book I'll be presenting a number of specific ideas for you to consider, grouped neatly into a range of subjects.

Clearly, one of the routes to living on less is spending less money. Again, there are a number of specific techniques highlighted in each chapter to help you achieve this, but in this section I'm going to introduce a set of generic tools that you can use to help reduce your daily expenditure. They will reappear throughout the book with more detailed information directly related to each topic.

The Shopping Revolution

The face of shopping has changed considerably since I was a child. The ways in which we acquire the goods and services we need or desire has undergone a bit of a revolution: credit cards now obviate the need to carry cash or cheque books; the Internet has crept up on us overnight, infiltrating just about every part of our lives; the look and feel of shops and financial institutions has gone through a complete overhaul. No more bank manager, Green Shield stamps or cheque guarantee cards, although there are some modern-day equivalents that have emerged to take their place. All these changes have been made in the name of convenience and in many cases economy but bit-by-bit, I fear we have been overcome by a deluge of modern habits and technologies that can make life ultra-convenient, and yet more expensive instead of easy and economic. Yes, the Internet, the credit card, the mega-store and the easy financing have given us more freedom, more choice and more purchasing power, but with this has come an easy way to spend money we don't actually have, frequently tempting us to over-indulge.

If we can avoid the pitfalls of our modern-day ultra-convenient shopping methods then we have at our fingertips a broad range of mechanisms that will support our goal of living on less. A key element to achieving a more frugal lifestyle is taking advantage of the wealth of deals and discounts, and being in the right place at the right time.

Strategy and Tactics

My husband, Ian, and I both love our holidays, so our principal living-on-less strategy is to make sure we take advantage of all the Internet deals offered for our holiday choices. During the year we build up Air Miles by converting our loyalty-card points so that we can exchange them for long-haul flights and accommodation (I think short-haul flights are often better catered for by budget airlines, particularly if you can book well in advance). How we achieve our holiday goals will become a bit of a theme throughout this book. Of course, saving Air Miles may not be your chosen goal – perhaps you want to save money for a specific event or simply need to live on less due to a change in circumstances that requires a lifestyle rethink. Whatever your goal, have a clear strategy and then consider which of the following living-on-less tactics are best suited for achieving your needs.

A Toolkit of Techniques for Living on Less

The following is a toolkit of techniques that will help you to live on less by taking advantage of the wealth of money-saving opportunities currently available. Look out for the "toolkit" symbol (⚒) throughout the book.

A TOOLKIT OF TECHNIQUES FOR LIVING ON LESS

Six of the Best: Toolkit and tactics for living on less.

- Budgeting and Planning – understanding your spending patterns; changing habits.
- Internet – taking advantage of a broad range of online money-saving opportunities.
- Credit vs Cash – selecting the right product and taking control of your finances.
- Shops and Outlets – getting to know your local environment.
- Timing – making your purchases by time of day/month/year or a particular season.
- Self-sufficiency – the ultimate mechanism for living on less: produce what you need yourself.

Budgeting and Planning

Budgeting

Reality Check: ϓ ϓ ① (£-)

Ian and I have always been good budgeters when it comes to big-ticket items, so we know that our top three annual expenses are (1) mortgage, (2) holidays and (3) groceries-including-wine. As we tend to be tied into a rolling medium-term (24 months) deal on the mortgage, we decided to look more closely at our holiday expenditure and food consumption to see what economies could be made. On top of our three principal expenses come the one-offs like new bathroom, landscaping, special events, plus all the other regular, everyday expenses.

Budgeting is easier and more enjoyable than you might think. Just writing down everything you spend money on is cathartic in itself – you'll be surprised at what you learn, so give it a go. Understanding where your money goes can be a real eye-opener. Once you know what you're spending your money on, and how much is being spent on each item every month, you can start to make simple economies.

If you want to create a budget, you could set up a simple table using traditional pen and paper, but there's quite a bit of adding up to do and grouping together of similar transactions so it would be better to buy a simple software package for the PC – we're currently using one that cost under a tenner from a high street supermarket, and it works as well as any professional package we've used in the past.

HOW TO LIVE ON LESS

Start by writing down your income and all the major items that you spend money on, for example:

Income
- Salary, bonus and any other income

Outgoings
- Mortgage and endowments
- Pension
- Utilities
- Education
- Healthcare
- Holidays, leisure and entertainment
- Groceries
- Computing, books and magazines
- Subscriptions – gym, charities, societies, etc.
- Insurance – car, life, home and contents
- Car – servicing, petrol, MoT
- Gifts
- Garden

Before long you end up with a long list of outgoings that add up to far more than your income – and that's why you have to learn to live on less!

Once your budget is set up, record each transaction as you make it – it only takes a few minutes each day to record the receipts you have gathered, or 30 minutes at the end of the week – and build a picture of your overall expenditure. From this you can generate an annual budget against which you can track the year's performance. There is something incredibly empowering about writing down all your expenditure. It provides insight and clarity to cash flow, and allows you to gain control. When you start to see just how much you spend on groceries, for example, it will make you think twice about buying ready-made meals or meat every day, plus it may give you the mental and moral boost to plan your weekly meals, buy only what you need for those meals, cook from scratch and/or become more self sufficient in the supply of foodstuffs – growing your own fruit and vegetables, possibly making your own alcoholic drinks.

A TOOLKIT OF TECHNIQUES FOR LIVING ON LESS

Think of your budgeting exercise as a financial makeover. Set a target of, say, £520 (divided, if you like, into easily-manageable chunks of £10 per week) that you want to save this year. Monitor your progress against the target, and then try something more ambitious next year. You should find you enjoy taking control and seeing results.

So that's the major expenditure nicely under control. However, it wasn't until I began research for this book that I started to look at where my *Cash* goes. Over the course of a week I made a quick note whenever I spent any cash and discovered I spent a staggering amount of money on caffé latte! At £1.80 at one venue and £2.30 at another, I'm spending on average £12.30 a week on cups of coffee, and that's almost £640 a year. That's particularly horrifying since we also have a superb coffee machine at home that does exactly the same thing. However, it doesn't have the girls from the gym to chat to at the same time, so I maintain that my expenditure is acceptable because it's part of my social life. I am making the positive choice of investing in time spent with my friends – and they're worth it (and I can justify just about anything if I really want to!). One of my girlfriends told me her top cash item was women's magazines, so she has decided to buy fewer and swap with one of the other girls, and for another it's chocolate bars. Both friends declined to tell me how much they spend – since I had already revealed my latte extravagance, I can only assume theirs was far, far worse...

Planning

Hand-in-hand with budgeting goes planning. Apart from everyday expenses, what else do you plan to spend money on this year and next? You may have some urgent household repairs or renovation that can't be left for another year, a special event to organise, or a new car. These need to be factored into your budget. Think about the timing of your purchases (see *Timing*, later) so that you can take advantage of the most opportune time. Also consider where you might buy your item – from an *Internet* source or a physical *Outlet* – and make sure you research their sales patterns.

It does mean that impulse buying becomes a thing of the past, but at least you will know you have got the best deal and are staying committed to your living-on-less strategy.

HOW TO LIVE ON LESS

Internet

Reality Check: ☥☥ ☺...☺☺ (£-) £+

Originally dubbed an "information super-highway", the Internet is now an important "savvy shopper's super-market"! And what a wealth of opportunities there are to search, compare, buy and sell if you only care to take a look. The Internet offers numerous mechanisms to help us live on less, but be careful – you can easily get distracted, so be focused on what you want to achieve and try not to go off on too many interesting tangents.

> Six of the Best: Internet techniques for living on less.
>
> - Online shopping
> - Cash-back portals
> - e-Trading
> - Social and business networks
> - Discount vouchers
> - Comparison websites

Online shopping. Just about any commodity can be bought or sold, transactions conducted, prices or models compared and information sought online. Online shopping is a superb living-on-less technique if you know exactly what you want, need bulky goods delivered, or you are shopping around for a good deal. The benefits of online shopping include ease of browsing, secure payment, a range of delivery options and the ability to avoid the crowds and the traffic. Note that when looking at the results of an Internet search, those that appear at the top of the page may not be the cheapest. Suppliers have often paid for the privilege of being high up on the list, so it's worth looking through several pages before making your selection.

Online prices are often cheaper than in-store as they cut out the middleman and the cost of a physical *Outlet*. Use your *Credit Card* (see later) combined with your *Loyalty Card* (see later) combined with a *Multi-purchase Deal* (see later) – you can even get additional money-off by using an online *Discount Voucher* (see later) or by accessing your selected shop through a *Cashback Portal* (see later). The following is not a definitive list, but here are some common activities that you might like to try online:

- banking
- books, music download, daily news, TV programmes, weather forecast

A TOOLKIT OF TECHNIQUES FOR LIVING ON LESS

- travel – rail, air, coach, ferry, holidays, hotels
- food and drink (what a pity you can't actually taste it online!)
- furniture and homeware
- theatre, leisure and sporting events tickets

Cashback Portals (or other rewards like Air Miles). These websites act as an "entrance hall" to your shopping and route you to hundreds of stores participating in their programme. When you purchase something from a participating store, your account is credited with cash or Air Miles or whatever is the reward scheme of your chosen portal. Numerous shopping "portals" (literally, gateways) usher you through their electronic doors armed with your *Credit Card*, potentially a *Loyalty Card*, and a fistful of *Discount Vouchers*, and entice you to spend, spend, spend. Each site typically requires a (free) subscription to join their programme. Stores participating in the programme pay back different levels of reward, and you may find the portal is offering an introductory gift of your chosen reward to get you started, or even a referral bonus if you introduce a new member. Drawbacks seem to be the thresholds at which payouts are made (you need to amass a specific amount of cashback or Air Miles before they are credited to you) and the initial delays in getting your first credits passed on to you.

In addition, it takes an awfully long time to build up a sensible amount of money, unless you are doing a lot of regular shopping online or purchasing expensive items like furniture. As with anything, check out a few sites before you select the one that's right for you. If you regularly shop online at Store X, why not check to see if they are part of a cashback (or other reward) portal – you could be losing out. See www.kelkoo.co.uk, www.myshoppingrewards.com and www.recordcashback.co.uk.

e-Trading. There are millions of ordinary people trading everyday items on the Internet, selling what they don't want or no longer need and looking out for a bargain that you might be offering.

- Auctions – buy as well as sell. It's amazing the range of products available on the e-trading websites and the prices are very compelling. Not all products are brand new, but generally the seller advises the state of the product and hopefully adjusts the price accordingly (or you can bid what you are willing to pay). You can usually purchase what you need for much less than from the high street stores. If selling, try to build up a good reputation by making purchases before you attempt

HOW TO LIVE ON LESS

to sell. When you come to sell, make sure you take a good picture of your item and provide useful information – check out what other people have done with similar products and select the best ideas for your own.

> ⓘ Did you know...? There is an interesting twist in online auctions that has started in Illinois (USA). The website www.4sale4now.com (which starts with a short introductory tutorial) provides an auction site where the price of goods actually goes down over time rather than up – very much akin to a Dutch auction. This overcomes the somewhat stressful process of bidding and means that if you are prepared to wait (and no-one else buys the goods before you do) you could purchase your desired item for up to 50% of the initial price. It really captures the spirit of bargain hunting.

- Community Networks – these are generally locally-organised groups that provide an online venue to exchange or give away goods and services.

  - Freecycle. You may be able to source exactly what you want, for free, on the local Freecycle network. Someone within a few miles of you may be advertising the very thing you need and only require that you pick it up from them. No payment sought or required – the ultimate living on less! Similarly, anything you no longer want that is in reasonably good nick can be offered through the site. If you do choose to use Freecycle, my advice is to select the "weekly digest" option if your group has one, otherwise you'll be inundated with e-mails...particularly if you opt to join several local groups. See www.freecycle.co.uk.
  - Local Exchange Trading Schemes (LETS) are local community-based mutual-aid networks in which people exchange all kinds of goods and services with one another, without the need for money but having direct exchange of "credits" – much as an early bartering system would have worked. You can earn a LETS credit by providing a service, and then spend the credits on whatever is offered by others in the scheme: for example, gardening, plumbing, childcare, transport, meals, the loan of equipment. There is no fixed list of services – it's just what you and the people in your area are able to offer. See www.letslinkuk.net.

Social and business networks. If you have already invested in a fixed-price broadband account, then the business and social networks represent

A TOOLKIT OF TECHNIQUES FOR LIVING ON LESS

a totally free communications tool that will keep you in touch, online, with your nearest and dearest as well as colleagues past and present. It's much more economical than using your landline or mobile phone to stay in touch and less intrusive on people's time. Keep up to date with what's happening in their lives and let them know about yours.

- Networks are based on "six degrees of separation", the well-known theory that each of us in the world is but six people apart.
- The business networks are focused and disciplined, and offer a useful mechanism for maintaining contact with colleagues and clients wherever they decide to move. They represent an invaluable networking tool.
- Social networks are great fun, and a free way to keep in contact with your friends and acquaintances.

Discount vouchers. See www.myvouchercodes.co.uk, www.captainconsumer.co.uk and www.promotionalcodes.org.uk for thousands of discount vouchers that can be used to reduce the price of your online shopping, or www.landoffreebies.co.uk for both discount vouchers and "freebies". Many vouchers expire after a short period of time, but you can receive an e-mail alert of any new vouchers that get posted. If you know what you want to buy, and from where, find a voucher to get a discount…or wait for one to become available before you proceed.

Comparison websites. These are a very useful starting point to many purchases. They have revolutionised the way we search, compare and buy products and services. They include not only commercial comparison sites but also consumer/watchdog sites, which will help you avoid purchasing "blind" by directing you through the maze of options, features, add-ons, etc. before you find what is right for you. No one site compares across the whole market, so it makes sense to "shop around" using several such sites to get a more universal view. Many companies, particularly banks, insurance, utilities, etc., have made money in the past through our own sloth – it's been so much easier to stick with our current supplier rather than go through the hassle of changing. Not so with the advent of the Internet and the numerous comparison websites. Check out a variety of prices from home insurance to gas bills to interest rates online, and change suppliers to get the best deals. However, don't forget to check with individual companies too – some offer price reductions if you go direct to them rather than through an intermediary, or you may be offered an improved deal if you already have existing business with that company.

HOW TO LIVE ON LESS

Credit vs Cash

> ⓘ Did you know…? In the last four years, UK purchases made with credit and debit cards exceeded purchases made with cash.

Reality Check: ♈♈ ①…①① (£-)

Cash. I've mentioned above the importance of keeping control over your cash by understanding exactly what you spend it on. But how about using cash positively as leverage for reducing the cost of your purchase? You might simply ask before you agree to buy, "What is your discount for cash"? It might be nothing, but you haven't ruined your opportunity to purchase at the original price just by asking. While the UK has not traditionally been a country where we haggle for every purchase, paying by cash does open up this opportunity. Bear in mind that you need to allow the supplier to make some profit at the same time as you negotiate a reduction in cost. But my view is, "Don't ask, don't get", and the worst the supplier can do is say "no" – you won't have lost anything by trying. Alternatively, and particularly in markets, you might try offering whatever money you do have to purchase something that's beyond your budget. My friend's daughter was keen to buy some jeans priced at £25 at a local market, but she had only £18 in her pocket. She told the stallholder this and the sale was made – the supplier is as keen to make a sale, even at reduced profit, rather than no sale at all, as you are to get a good deal.

On the downside, cash does not have the purchase protection that credit cards do: this insurance safeguards goods against accidental damage, theft or robbery up to 100 days after the purchase.

Credit Card. Plastic fantastic? Friend or foe? A useful tool for living on less, or a huge spending trap?

As credit card usage becomes more complex, yet more convenient, we now have a range of options to pay for goods and services, either at the checkout or online. No need for signatures, no need to speak to anyone, tap in four digits and it's done – so quick, so easy, so be careful… The trouble is, since using a credit card is psychologically different to paying with hard cash, there is a tendency to spend money you don't actually have, and possibly never will, such that running up a debt is quickly done. If you had to hand over the equivalent amount of cash for the purchases you make on credit card, would you actually do it? I am not suggesting you carry vast amounts

A TOOLKIT OF TECHNIQUES FOR LIVING ON LESS

of cash around with you – it's not practical – but credit cards may not help us live on less unless they are used with due care and attention.

I prefer to pay off the whole bill each time the credit card invoice arrives, but I know many who pay the absolute minimum and thus are paying through the nose on interest to the credit card company (and that's got to be a huge waste of money, not to mention lining someone else's pocket!). Credit card debt not only zaps your financial strength but it just makes you miserable. I'm not a debt advisor, but my view is if you can't pay off the whole bill, then at least pay off more than the minimum required or if you can't stop spending then cut the damn things up so they're not available. The most important thing is: take control!

There are basically three ways of using a credit card: straightforward purchases, moving an outstanding debt over from another card (balance transfer), and withdrawing cash from a hole-in-the-wall. Withdrawing cash generally incurs a cash-handling fee in addition to interest, which increases the cost to you; conversely, several cards offer 0% interest on balance transfers for a limited period. Keep a note of when your deal expires, and if you haven't cleared your debt by the end of that period (or cannot) then move to another 0% card. One option is to use a different credit card for each different purpose, though personally I wouldn't use a credit card to get cash – much better to use a debit card which is interest-free while you're in credit.

Comparing credit cards has become easier since regulation has required companies to come clean with their information. See *Comparison Websites* (above). Select your credit cards wisely according to how they will benefit you the most. Several cards give either cashback, vouchers, limited-period zero interest or loyalty points. If your credit card provides you with loyalty points, make sure they are interchangeable with other *Loyalty Schemes* (see later) you belong to and change your card (or your loyalty scheme) if not.

Direct debit. A quick word on direct debit while we're considering credit vs cash. If you don't already pay by direct debit for your regular bills, then do check with your supplier, as they often give an improved tariff for direct debit over cheque payments. Direct debit also helps *Budgeting and Planning*, as it is often possible to pay a fixed amount each month, thus spreading the cost evenly over the year. However, don't fall into the trap of having direct debits for "dead" requirements – maybe a subscription you no longer want?

HOW TO LIVE ON LESS

Shops and Outlets

Reality Check: ☂ ☺...☺☺ (£-)

Out-of-town superstores, city-centre mega-stores, oversized supermarkets – they all now sell clothes, PCs, homeware; department stores now sell groceries; most of the larger shops provide a café or a restaurant; and if we want the diversity and choice, a shopping mall provides the perfect warm, covered environment to dip in and out of or favourite retailers – we can stay in the same place all day if we want! Great for getting all your shopping in one place, but it means taking the car, using up fuel, potentially not allowing us to "market" for the best quality, but ultimately giving us good value products. If you have the time it's worth getting to know several shops and what items they sell for less – swap ideas with your friends. Factory outlet stores are often a good venue for getting cut-price goods, if they are genuine: I find some outlets sell poor-quality goods and sometimes goods that are not discounted at all.

Charity shops, car boot sales, single-price "value retailers", budget supermarkets.

- I suppose I'd be showing my age if I added jumble sales to the list?
- Charity shops are a very useful source of cheaper items. Sadly I think the shops could use an injection of style into their display but believe me, you can pick up a real bargain. I have found that the charity shops in more affluent towns and cities have superior items. Don't forget to donate your own unwanted goods to the shop for them to sell.
- Car boot sales are great venues for purchasing good value items as well as making a few extra pounds if you want to de-clutter your home and have a stall of your own.
- Single-price value retailers can be your most economical way of buying everyday items, but you do need to be a savvy shopper. If you are buying soap, the supermarket may just have a buy-one-get-one-free (BOGOF) or 3-for-2 offer that beats the single-price shop. You just have to know…

> ⓘ Did you know…? There has also been an explosion of single-price value retailers on the continent. But beware the exchange rate…currently those shops are selling everything for Euro 1.25…our £1 or even 90p might just be better value…

A TOOLKIT OF TECHNIQUES FOR LIVING ON LESS

Own brand. I'm probably just as guilty as anyone of buying branded products, and I know that it's sometimes difficult to get your family to change. However, there really are better deals to be had if you buy own brand goods, so this is an important element to living on less.

Multi-purchase Deals like BOGOF and their cousins "3 for 2", "buy one get one half price", etc. These are the sales promotions reported as being the most effective forms of special offer for goods. As we are considering specifically how to live on less, I feel I cannot get into any arguments about who loses out in the buy-one-get-one-free value chain. Rest assured, someone does. However, it's one of the handiest tools for living on less if we can multi-buy products cheaply; though conversely it's a spending trap if you buy two of something when you only need one. You need discipline and control to make this tactic work for you. Typically these deals are available for books, DVDs, foodstuffs and toiletries, but they are fast becoming popular for clothing.

> ① Did you know...? In 2008 even car dealers jumped on the BOGOF bandwagon – one commented that they had attempted to sell individual cars at half price with only some success, but their BOGOF campaign crashed the company website. The deal was such a huge success they are planning to do another one in the future.

Loyalty Schemes – used by airlines, DIY and garden centres, department stores, supermarkets, coffee shops, petrol stations to name but a few – encourage you to continue shopping with them by offering an incentive such as a future discount or gift. For the retailer it's a very effective brand-loyalty and customer-retention marketing tool that rewards and encourages loyal buying behaviour. Loyalty cards typically use a points system – and points mean prizes! – that build up to money off the final bill or in-store vouchers, or can be traded for other partner credits, e.g. Air Miles. The retailer gets valuable demographic information about us every time we swipe our loyalty card. The items we have bought are recorded and provide the store with a mechanism to target us with offers for high-profit goods. (No need to be fearful of National ID cards – we already have them!) They also use the information to group products on shelves to entice us to spend more.

I have numerous loyalty cards – it takes a while to sift through them to get to the one I want. Some give me the opportunity to take money off the cost of my purchases at the till, others send a voucher for use in the store, and several allow me to convert to Air Miles (more holidays!) or to have discounted leisure activities. The most difficult thing I find is remembering who is partnered with whom. I need to create a list or even a mini-database to keep a record so that I can take best advantage of the schemes. You will probably be a member of a different set of loyalty schemes to me, but for the record I've got cards for:

- garden centres (3)
- supermarkets (2)
- airlines (3)
- hotel chains (3)
- homeware/DIY stores (3)
- department stores (2)
- stationery and art stores (3)
- coffee shops (2)

Discounts and discount vouchers. Like their online equivalents, discount vouchers are a key element to living on less *if you use them to buy something you regularly purchase*. Numerous stores now provide their own magazine and they are often littered with discount vouchers (as are many national newspapers and magazines) that you cut out and hand in at the checkout desk. Save the ones you know you will use and leave the rest behind. If you are a member of an institution – gym, Royal Horticultural Society, National Trust, Institute of Directors, etc. – or have a railcard, make sure you are aware of the discounts available to you through them.

Duty- and tax-free outlets and other overseas purchases. If you are a frequent overseas traveller, get to know the relative cost of items available in the various duty- and tax-free outlets (taking into account fluctuations in the exchange rate). If your travel additionally allows time to go shopping locally, keep an eye out for items that you would normally buy in the UK that are sourced in the country you are visiting. They may well be cheaper. My husband is great for getting the best deals on gin (oops, now I'm revealing another vice!); I myself know the best places to buy my favourite perfume, moisturisers and sunscreen. Whenever we need electrical goods, the tax- and duty-free outlet prices are factored into our planning, comparison checking and budgeting. If you are planning a big party and need a quantity of alcohol, why not mix a fun day out with a "booze cruise" – with good forward *Planning* you can get a great deal on a cross-channel ferry or the Chunnel to pick up bargains on the continent.

A TOOLKIT OF TECHNIQUES FOR LIVING ON LESS

Auctions. The original and physical equivalent to online auctions, auction houses are an exciting way to buy and sell products, and with care and discipline can help you live on less. Just about any commodity can be bought at auction – artwork, houses, furniture, jewellery – you just need to know what the focus of the auction is going to be. Check out the catalogue and sale items in advance, set yourself a budget, then get bidding. Discipline is needed not to exceed your budget. As well as buying, hopefully for less, you can also sell your own goods. You might want to set a reserve price so that an item does not get undersold. Remember, people attending auctions aren't necessarily buying for their own use; they may be looking for bargains that they can sell on for a profit at a later auction.

Timing

Reality Check: ♈ ①…①①① (£-)

Timing your purchase may be critical. For example, some of the budget airlines offer significant savings if you book well in advance; conversely, you may get an excellent deal if you can wait until the last minute for theatre tickets or package holidays.

I've mentioned both online and paper discount vouchers above. If you are prepared to wait and keep an eye on websites and the press (or sign up for an e-mail alert) you could get a discount voucher to support your particular purchase – the trouble is you can't predict the timing of the discount voucher, nor the scope and terms of the deal.

We had an interesting experience. Ian needed a new car and it was July. The timing hadn't been planned, it was just how it happened to work out. The salesman was very keen to sell him a car. He spent time with him going through the various models, kicking the tyres, explaining the financial packages on offer (some very compelling deals in themselves!), taking him out on an extended test drive, etc. It turned out, happily, that it was the end of the salesman's half-year and he needed extra sales to meet targets. He was able to offer an attractive discount and a really great financial package so long as we purchased before the end of the month. We got the car we wanted, cheaper than expected; the salesman made his sale, and presumably achieved his commission target. Everyone went home happy.

Self-sufficiency

Reality Check: ϒ... ϒ ϒ ϒ ①...①②③ (£-)...£££- £+...£££+ ♥

By far the most effective mechanism for living on less is to become self-sufficient in the services or products you need on a regular basis. In some cases this could mean a complete change of lifestyle, in others a new installation or possibly a specific change in the way you behave. For example, investing in solar panels and/or a wind vane to generate your own electricity is mildly invasive and fairly costly, but could mean you would be free from the national grid. At the other end of the scale, you could take up walking to improve your health and fitness, and combine it with foraging for wild greens, berries and fungi. Food for free is the ultimate in living on less (so long as you know what you're doing). Each of the chapters of this book has a section dedicated to self-sufficiency. You will see just how easy it could be to live on less by becoming self-sufficient in a few areas of your life (e.g. growing vegetables or raising chickens), or it could just encourage you to make long-term changes in order to make more significant savings.

chapter 2

Energy, Water and Fuel

Green is the colour: frugal is the game! Reducing the amount of energy we use or investing in mechanisms to use free, renewable energy like the wind and the sun not only helps us to live on less, it also has the added bonus of being more eco-friendly – it may not be easy being green, but every little helps!

Electricity

Saving Money on Electricity

Reality Check: ϒ ☺ £- ♥

Since we pay for every unit of electricity we use, reducing the amount of energy we consume on a daily basis means we can immediately live on less. It can be as simple as turning off a light switch or turning down the thermostat to investing in home insulation and energy-efficient appliances. In fact, saving money on energy could be achieved simply by selecting the right supplier.

> ⓘ Did you know...? If you're happy to have an online electricity account, you could immediately save yourself some money. We looked at www.uswitch.com and discovered we could save £283.49 a year just by switching supplier.

🛠 Once upon a time (when gas was supplied only by a nationalised gas company) we stayed with our utility supplier for life because there was no other choice. Deregulation has opened the market to more companies and given us a wealth of options and a confusing set of deals. Just as sloth and greed are the enemies of the stock exchange, so now we need to give due consideration to when and whether to change our utility supplier in order to get the best deals. The *Comparison Websites* that have sprung up over the last few years demonstrate exactly what is on offer and can generally be tailored to our precise requirements, making it easy to change and stay ahead of the game. Several utility suppliers also offer an improved deal if you allow them to supply all your utilities, though this may be dependent upon your location.

🛠 In addition, swap to a *Direct Debit* payment mechanism if you currently use cheque – several suppliers offer a discount for direct debit and it will additionally help with your *Budgeting and Planning.*

ⓘ Did you know...? In the UK we're using twice the amount of electricity we did in the 1970s, and that figure is set to rise a further 12% in the next three years.

Immediate cost savings as well as positive environmental impact can be gained simply by reducing the amount of power we use around the home.

🛠 To improve electricity *Budgeting and Planning* and generally understand more about how your household uses and consumes electricity, why not fit a monitor? Better still from a living-on-less perspective, rent a monitor for a short time while you educate yourself and the family before taking remedial action. There are a number of easy-to-use electricity monitoring tools on the market which will allow you to take either a one-off snapshot or a longer-term view of exactly where electricity is being consumed and how much you are spending hour by hour. Get the family involved in checking the monitor readings and converting this to a price per hour. If they can see the correlation between usage and expense (particularly if you need to trade off paying for computer usage against saving for a weekend break or tickets to a football match), they will take more interest in reducing the amount of energy the household uses. Once you understand which electrical appliances use the most electricity, and when, you can take remedial action if you want.

ENERGY, WATER AND FUEL

Six of the Best: Practical ideas to reduce the amount of electricity we use on a daily basis.

- Don't leave appliances on, or on standby – leaving your PC on overnight is like leaving three lights on in the house, though most have a sleep mode – and remember not to leave appliances on charge unnecessarily. Take at look at www.byebyestandy.co.uk for a neat piece of kit that allows you to cut power to appliances such as televisions and computers remotely at a flick of a switch – turn off when you turn in at night. We're really happy with the pair we installed in the lounge, managed by a single remote control device, to switch off our entertainment systems (a pretentious description for our ageing TV, DVD, CD, VHS, Freeview box and amplifier). We ought to fit the same devices to our PC and computer peripherals too, but one of us always has something open (unsaved!) on the PC that we wouldn't want to lose. (I am making a mental note as I write to become more disciplined at saving my work!)
- Fill up the washing machine, tumble dryer or dishwasher whenever you can. If not, use the half-load or economy programme. However, a half-load programme uses more than half the energy and water of a full load. If your freezer isn't full, plug the spaces with crumpled newspaper to make sure it runs at optimum efficiency, or take advantage of supermarket *Multi-Purchase Deals* to fill available space with foodstuffs.
- Washing at 30ºC instead of 40ºC reduces electricity consumption by around 40% – line-drying clothes in the garden rather than in a drier further saves energy and is of course absolutely free.
- Fit a "Savaplug" to your fridge and freezer – it will sense the reduced need for current when the motor isn't running at full power and reduce the flow of electricity, and therefore the cost to you, to match the actual requirements – see www.capcarbon.co.uk.
- Always turn off the lights when you leave a room – and make sure they are energy-saving bulbs.
- Only boil as much water in a kettle as you need, and make sure you put a lid on saucepans when you are cooking.

✘ If you are able to change the *Timing* of any of your electrical appliance usage (particularly dishwasher and washing machine), then energy used overnight is generally cheaper than daytime – check your tariff to see whether there is a difference. However, current wisdom suggests that the elderly or infirm should not use this tactic in case there are problems during the night, which they cannot easily attend to.

HOW TO LIVE ON LESS

Self-sufficiency: Generating Electricity

Completely replacing your current supply and becoming self-sufficient in the production of electricity is significantly more difficult – and more expensive – to achieve and, while the idea of being completely independent of the national grid may sound compelling, for many households it is unlikely to be a serious option. However, if you do generate your own electricity supply then it may be worth maintaining a link back to the grid to import what you need when your own system isn't working, and to sell back any surplus supply.

Micro-generation Systems

It is possible to become self-sufficient in generating electricity for the household using one or more micro-generating systems, which use free and renewable sources of energy – from the sun, the wind or water – to convert into electricity. You will need to weigh up the costs and Time to Break Even and reach an informed decision. Of course, financial considerations may not be your only influencing factor; for example, you may be keen to reduce the use of fossil fuels and their impact on the environment.

Other advantages of micro-generation include:

- If desired, you can be independent from the mains supply, in which case storage facilities such as batteries can be used.
- Alternatively you can stay linked to the mains supply, to provide a backup and/or sell surplus electricity back to the grid.
- Energy is generated on site, so there are no transmission losses due to distance as there are with national suppliers.
- Generating your own energy highlights your awareness of exactly how much energy you use, and therefore makes you use it more efficiently.

Harnessing Solar Energy

Reality Check: ϒ ϒ ☺☺ £££- £+ ♥

> ① Did you know...? You can buy solar-powered gadgets to use the sun's free, renewable energy to power mobile phone chargers or iPods.

There are two types of "solar panel": those which heat water or our living space, which we'll come to later in the chapter, and those that generate electricity, which I'm going to cover in this section.

ENERGY, WATER AND FUEL

Solar panels used for generating electricity are more accurately called Photovoltaic (PV) Cells (from the Greek photon, meaning light, and the unit of electrical potential, the volt). PV cells could provide up to half your electricity needs – sufficient at least for lighting and running appliances. All they need to work is daylight. Direct sunlight is not actually required, although the greater the intensity of sunlight, the greater the flow of electricity – and to achieve this you need a roof that has around 3–4 m^2 within 90° of South, without any obstruction. There is an obvious drawback that you can't generate electricity at night.

You can purchase PV arrays in a number of shapes and colours. Some look exactly like roof tiles – a good option if you need to replace some tiles, or have a complete new roof to install. Others are transparent and therefore suitable for conservatories. The electricity generated by PV cells is direct current (DC) at low voltage, suitable for running low-voltage DC appliances. If you need to use 240 V AC, then you'll also need to buy an inverter.

Output from PV arrays is measured at the peak rate of production, known as kWp – kilowatts produced at peak. Prices for PV systems vary, depending on what you choose to install, but for the average domestic system you'd be talking about £5,000–£8,000 per kWp installed; typically households use between 1.5 and 3 kWp.

PV panels generate most of their electricity during the daytime, when domestic demand is generally low, thus the opposite of what is needed. Surplus electricity which is not used in the household can then be sold back to the electricity supplier (see Sell-Back section). During the time when the panels are not generating, electricity will have to be imported and paid for as normal. Generally this requires two-way metering. Not all suppliers offer this and charges and prices vary. In some case the charges may have a significant impact on the Time to Break Even.

Grants
Around 8.5 million pounds in grant money had been paid by November 2008 (all UK) on 5924 installations across all technologies – an average of £1,350 per installation. Statistics are provided on the low carbon buildings website (see below).

You may be entitled to a grant to install a PV system.

In England, Wales and Northern Ireland grants are administered through the Low Carbon Buildings Programme (part of the Department for Business Enterprise and Regulatory Reform), who aim to process claims within 25 days. See www.lowcarbonbuildings.org.uk.

The grant for PV systems could be up to £2,000 per kWp, with an overall maximum grant of £2,500 or 50% of the relevant eligible costs, whichever is the lower. Grant validity is four months for installation in an existing building and six months for those under construction.

In Scotland, grants are administered under the Scottish Community and Householder Renewables Initiative (SCHRI).
See www.energysavingstrust.org.uk/scotland.

Grants of up to 30% of the costs for PV systems are available to householders, up to a maximum of £4,000.

Note that in Northern Ireland the Reconnect programme closed to new grant applications on 31st March 2008.

Time to Break Even
The Time to Break Even is the amount of time it takes for the cost of the installation to be repaid through savings in fuel bills.

For the sake of convenience and to simplify the calculation, I have made the following assumptions:

- The inflation rate on fuel and the lost bank interest due to making a large capital investment cancel each other out and have been removed from the calculation. I personally think this is a bit pessimistic, but in the interest of simplicity let's proceed without them.
- An inverter is not required to convert DC to AC, so has not been factored into the cost.
- Potential income from the sale of surplus electricity has not reduced the overall cost.
- The VAT on renewable energy remains at the reduced rate of 5%.

ENERGY, WATER AND FUEL

Looking at my own electricity bill, I have three different tariffs (inclusive of VAT):

Day primary	24.22p per kWh
Day secondary	10.31p per kWh
Night	4.65p per kWh

I will be using the "Day Secondary" figure to calculate the Time to Break Even. This tariff is used once the "Day Primary" threshold is exceeded, and is the rate at which 70% of my electricity is charged.

PV System cost including: • PV array • installation	£6,500
Government grant (1 kWp)	£2,000
VAT at 5% on £6,500	£325
Gross cost	PV System minus grant plus VAT £6,500 − £2,000 + £325 = £4,825
Peak system output	1 kWp
Amount of electricity produced	Ave 2 hours per day x 365 days x 1 kW = 912.5 kWh
Price of electricity (my most-used tariff)	10.31p per kWh = £0.1031
Annual saving	Electricity produced times price of electricity 912.5 x £0.1031 = £94.08
Time to Break Even	Gross cost divided by annual saving £4,825 / £94.08 = 51 years 4 months

Planning Permission

In England, changes to permitted development rights for domestic micro-generation technologies introduced on 6th April 2008 have lifted the requirements for planning permission for most solar PV installations. Roof-mounted and stand-alone systems can now be installed in most dwellings, as long as they respect certain size criteria.

In Wales, Scotland and Northern Ireland, governments are currently all considering changes to their legislation on permitted developments, to facilitate installations of micro-generation technologies, including solar PV. Until then, householders in Wales, Scotland and Northern Ireland must consult with their local authority regarding planning permission.

HOW TO LIVE ON LESS

Selling Your Excess Electricity Back to the Grid (Sell-back)
The situation with Sell-back is changing continuously and differs from supplier to supplier. If you intend to go down this route I suggest doing your homework and shopping around. In some cases, the supplier simply does not agree to purchase domestically produced surplus electricity. In other cases, the supplier may elect to purchase your surplus at the same price they sell electricity to you – this is called net metering. Others offer to buy at a substantially reduced tariff, say 50%, because they are able to purchase electricity more cheaply on the wholesale market. Whatever the final agreed price, you will need to install a replacement meter, which in itself will not be an insignificant cost, and could just be the straw that breaks the camel's back, particularly if your surplus is a small quantity.

Wind Turbines

> ⓘ Did you know…? Britain is by far the windiest country in Europe – we get about 40% of Europe's wind – yet Spain has five times the number of wind farms we do.

Reality Check: ⛏ ⛏ ☺☺ £££- £+ ♥

Until the day we moved into our current house, my husband and I had never considered owning a wind turbine. We had seen tiny wind vanes used very successfully on pleasure yachts to generate small amounts of electricity, but the idea somehow didn't transfer to a domestic situation. Our location is open to the elements from all sides and the wind seems to funnel its way straight to us, so the opportunity to generate some of our electricity needs from harnessing wind power is quite compelling. Seven years on and we still don't have a wind turbine, but we have been keeping an eye on the market, doing our research and waiting for other more pressing (interesting?) projects like the kitchen, the garden and the vegetable patch to finish absorbing precious time and cash flow.

How Can We Turn Wind Power Into Electricity?
Micro wind turbines harness the wind's free and renewable forces to turn blades that power a rotor to create electricity. It's that simple! The amount of electricity you actually generate depends on the length of the rotor blades, the wind speed and a few other factors. Suddenly it's not so simple! For the technical among you, I can provide a nice equation to illustrate this ratio:

ENERGY, WATER AND FUEL

The power (P) of a wind turbine is proportional to the length of the rotor blades and to the cube of the wind speed (v):

$$P = \tfrac{1}{2} \alpha \, \rho \, \pi r^2 \, v^3$$

In this equation, P = power in watts, α = a capacity factor determined by the design of the turbine, ρ = air density in kilograms per cubic metre, r = radius of the wind turbine in metres, and v = wind speed in metres per second.

What this means is that if you have a wind turbine whose rotor blades have a 2 m diameter, you will get four times as much energy as one with only 1 m diameter. Similarly, the wind has only to increase from 5 m/s to 6 m/s to nearly double the amount of power generated. However, it's not possible to harness all the available power from the wind – there would be nothing left to rustle through the trees or dry your clothes if you did – and it's generally considered that the limit is about half. This is the capacity factor.

When you take a look at the different wind turbines on the market, you will see that they are rated by comparing their output to a wind speed of 12 m/s – equivalent to 27 mph (and that's a pretty windy day) – which is the speed at which they can generate 1 kW of electricity. Now, we do get winds that strong, but it's not exactly typical nor is it guaranteed, so you will have to assume that your wind turbine will generally not be operating to its full efficiency. In fact, below 3 m/s there will be no power generated, and when it blows a hooley an automatic safety cutout kicks in to make sure the turbine doesn't run amok.

Other factors that will contribute to the efficiency of your wind turbine include:

- where you live in UK
- proximity to other buildings, trees, etc.
- turbulence
- height of your wind turbine

Urban environments do not always lend themselves to good wind turbine locations for the above reasons. You may live in a geographic location that is simply not windy enough, or maybe it's too windy; the other buildings around you might force the wind to bypass you altogether or cause so much turbulence that it makes power generation impossible; or you simply may not be able to get your turbine high enough, given the need to clear local obstructions. I recommend you engage a qualified professional to determine whether your site is suitable for a wind turbine generator before you go ahead and purchase.

Wind, like the rain, comes and goes as it pleases, day or night, sometimes both. Thus electricity will be generated at these times – great if you need the electricity when the wind blows, tough if you don't. At least there is a chance with wind-generated electricity that we can have an output around the clock – unlike solar energy, which can be a daylight provider only. An alternative source of energy is therefore still needed, although excess electricity can be sold back to the grid (see Sell-Back under Harnessing Solar Energy, above).

So how much does it all cost? Systems up to 1 kW will cost as little as £1,500 but if you want to generate, say, 6 kW then you could be talking £25,000 installed. These costs are inclusive of the turbine, mast, inverters, battery storage (if required) and installation. Once installed you should expect your turbine to last for about 20 years, assuming you keep it maintained to ensure it continues to operate effectively. For battery storage systems, typical battery life is around 6–10 years, depending on the type, so batteries may have to be replaced at some point in the system's life.

Grants
See the Grants section in Harnessing Solar Energy for general information on grants and website details of the government agencies.

In England, Wales and Northern Ireland grants are available for wind turbines to cover up to a maximum of £1,000 per kWp installed, with an overall maximum of £2,500 or 30% of the relevant eligible costs, whichever is the lower. Grant validity is four months for installation in an existing building and six months for those under construction.

In Scotland, the grant is currently set at 30% of the installed cost of a renewable measure, up to £4,000.

Time to Break Even
For the sake of convenience and to simplify the calculation, I have made the following assumptions:

ENERGY, WATER AND FUEL

- The inflation rate on fuel and the lost bank interest due to making a large capital investment cancel each other out and have been removed from the calculation.
- Potential income from the sale of surplus electricity has not reduced the cost.
- The VAT on renewable energy remains at the reduced rate of 5%.

Net cost of wind turbine, including: • turbine, mast, inverters, battery storage • installation	£1,500
Government grant (30% of relevant eligible cost)	£450
VAT at 5% on £1,500	£75
Gross cost	Net cost minus grant plus VAT £1,500 − £450 + £75 = £1125
System output at 12 m/s (27 mph)	1 kW
Amount of electricity produced pa	Ave 2½ hours per day x 365 days x 1 kW = 912.5 kWh
Price of electricity (my most-used tariff)	10.31p per kWh = £0.1031
Annual saving	Amount of electricity times price of electricity 912.5 * £0.1031 = £94.08
Time to Break Even	Gross cost divided by annual saving = £1125 / £94.08 = 12 years

Planning Permission

Planning permission is currently (January 2009) required for mini wind turbines.

Micro-hydro

Water can be harnessed as a reliable and consistent means of generating electricity that operates constantly throughout the day and night. Useful power can be converted from even the smallest stream – the running water drives a turbine or waterwheel to produce electricity. The amount of power you can extract from a body of water depends on the water's flow rate (per second) and the height (or head) that the water falls. A good hydro system can generate a steadier, more reliable electricity supply than other renewable technologies at a lower cost. Like PV and wind turbines, hydro-electric power systems can be independent of the grid system or linked into it.

The hydroelectric power in a stream or river can be calculated as follows:

Hydro power (kW) = head (m) x flow (m^3/s) x acceleration due to gravity (9.81 m/s/s)

For example, if the head is 2.50 m and the available flow is 0.15 m^3/s, the hydroelectric power is:

2.50 x 0.15 x 9.81 = 3.68 kW

At 50% equipment efficiency, in this example the turbine would generate electricity at the rate of 1.84 kW. Depending on the degree of sophistication, water turbine efficiencies can be as high as 90%.

Grants

See the Grants section in Harnessing Solar Energy for general information on grants and website details of the government agencies.

In England, Wales and Northern Ireland grants are available for micro-hydro systems to cover up to a maximum of £1,000 per kWp installed, with an overall maximum of £2,500 or 30% of the relevant eligible costs, whichever is the lower. Grant validity is 12 months for installations in both existing buildings and those under construction.

In Scotland, the grant is currently set at 30% of the installed cost of a renewable measure, up to £4,000.

Heating

Saving Money: Conserving Heat

Heating has to be one of the biggest energy thieves in our homes, and that means we could be wasting money by overheating our rooms and/or losing heat through poor insulation. Around 60% of our energy bill is spent on heating the space we live in (quite apart from heating water, which takes up probably another 25% of domestic energy…see later), so it is well worth looking at ways of conserving our heat, reducing that expenditure and potentially even generating our own heating source.

There are some easy steps to reducing heating bills, as well as the option to adopt new technology for longer-term self-sufficiency in heating water

ENERGY, WATER AND FUEL

and space. However, in the short term it's more cost-effective to spend a little effort and money retaining what heat we have – i.e. not losing any through poor insulation, or wasting any through simply over-heating the house or having an inefficient boiler – before considering any investment in heat generation from renewable, sustainable energy sources.

Insulation

Reality Check: ϒ ϒ ☺☺ £- ♥

If you live in a brand new dwelling, chances are the house has been designed and built with all the modern forms of insulation that are available – loft, floor, cavity wall, double glazing, lagged tank, etc. – but older properties, and even those only 5–10 years old, may be leaking heat literally from floor to roof. You may even have all the recommended forms of insulation installed in your home, but not a sufficient level – recent guidelines suggest loft insulation, for example, needs to be around 27 cm (10") deep, and the lagging around the hot water cylinder at least 75 mm (3") thick. Pop up to your loft and tank and check out the thickness of your insulation and take remedial action if necessary.

It is estimated that it costs two or three times more to heat an uninsulated home than it does a modern home – the biggest culprits for heat loss being walls and loft – so for many of us there are instant living-on-less opportunities just from ensuring we reduce heat losses by improving our insulation.

Reducing Heat Loss
Where I sit in my home office is now a comfortable working temperature, even in the winter. But it wasn't always like this. We bought the house seven years ago as a renovated and extended property, but during the first winter it was clear there were a number of cold draughts that needed to be fixed. We hadn't particularly noticed this during the summer – a shame we had to wait until the coldest part of the year to become aware of the problem, but perhaps you can learn from our mistakes. All the windows were thankfully OK, but if you put your hand up against the French doors or at the base of the door leading to the garage, there was enough fresh air coming in to warrant drying clothes in front of them.

Have a look around the edges of any windows or doors where draughts are occurring to see whether they meet their frames properly or if there is any warping in one area. If there isn't a tight fit all the way round, you could add self-adhesive strips inside the closure. If there is obvious warping, then PVC door strips are a better choice. The bottoms of doors can be fitted with a brush strip. These fulfil the dual purpose of improving insulation and sweeping the floor clean as you open and close it. We also use one of those old-fashioned "sausage dog" draught excluders placed along the inner edge of the door, mainly because there is a difference in height between two rooms, and the strip insulation is insufficiently thick to make a tight closure.

> Six of the Best: Practical ideas to reduce heat loss around the home.
>
> - One-third of building heat is lost through walls – cavity wall insulation is relatively cheap to install and could save you around £90 per year.
> - If you don't have it already, install double glazing – it can cut heat loss through windows by up to 50%.
> - Deal with any open vents or wall penetrations that are not used to expel humidity. Common ones include the letterbox, gaps in the skirting board and an open chimney – it was easy to board our chimney over and we are not currently using our fireplace. Vents in the kitchen and bathroom should not be covered as you may end up with a bad case of mould from constant condensation that can't escape.
> - You may have insulated the loft itself, but what about the loft hatch? If there is a gap around the hatch and you can feel the cool air coming into the house, fix it with self-adhesive strips.
> - Fit an insulating jacket over your hot water tank.
> - Closing your curtains in the evening stops heat escaping through the windows – don't forget to include those rooms you're not occupying.

Your local DIY store will be able to advise what products you can use – and you can start saving money immediately.

Thermostat Level

My father was a great believer in "put on an extra jumper rather than lighting the fire" and indeed when I was a girl there wasn't the option to just flick on the switch of an electric fire – either you lit a fire in the grate in the lounge, or you didn't. Typically, therefore, we had a lot of jumpers…

Reality Check: (👕) (🕐) (£-) ❤

ENERGY, WATER AND FUEL

> ⓘ **Did You Know...?** Turning the thermostat down by 1°C could reduce your heating consumption by about 10% – that could be anything from £30 to £75 saving per year, dependent on the size of your house. Also, your hot water may just be too hot – another waste of energy as well as your money! Your cylinder thermostat shouldn't need to be set higher than 60°C (140°F).

It still makes sense to wear something extra rather than turning the heating on or up, but you do need to feel comfortable. As I work in my home office, with windows on three aspects, I am cosy in a sweatshirt, jeans and socks (or even in my dressing-gown first thing in the morning), but I refuse to go any further and wear hat, gloves and a scarf. I am in my home after all, working, and I want to be comfortable. So instead of putting on the central heating when it gets a bit chilly during the day, I just have a mini-fan-heater that gives a short burst of heat if ever I need it.

Any room where you work or sit for any length of time does need to be at a sensible temperature – say around 21°C – but other rooms like bedrooms, cloakrooms and rooms that naturally warm up like kitchens and utilities can operate comfortably at around 18°C. These temperatures may need to be adjusted when accommodating the very elderly, young or infirm. Check your thermostat, or the individual radiator settings, and make adjustments where you can.

Boiler Efficiency

Just as a kettle gets lime scale build-up, so does your boiler. Regular maintenance is essential – a service every year is recommended – as flushing the sludge out of the boiler will help it to run more efficiently.

If you are considering changing the boiler (and you should if yours is 15 years old or more), you will almost certainly be buying a condensing boiler. These boilers condense water vapour as part of the combustion process, recovering heat at the same time. Condensing boilers achieve efficiencies of around 90% (as compared to a regular boiler, which is about 75% efficient). According to the Energy Saving Trust, a new condensing boiler could save you around a third on your heating bill, and that could be at least £100 per year, if not more. Have a look at their website for more information: www.energysavingtrust.org.uk.

Self-sufficiency: Generating Heat

Solar Thermal Systems

Reality Check: ⚡ ☺☺ £££- ♥

> ⓘ Did You Know...? A solar thermal heater could be linked up to an underfloor heating system. As underfloor heating operates at lower temperatures than radiator-based systems, it is well suited to the lower temperatures obtainable from solar thermal heaters.

You can buy either solar tubes or flat plates to collect the energy from the sun to heat water and typically generate up to half of your water heating needs. If you need to replace part of your roof, or are putting a new roof in (e.g. for an extension) this might be a good time to install a solar thermal system. The sun's power is, of course, a free and totally renewable source of energy, and it is available pretty much year round. You don't need very much winter sun to raise water temperature, and in fact most of the energy required to heat water is used to take it from cold to lukewarm. A smaller amount of energy is then required to raise the temperature to that which is comfortable for a bath or shower – a regular boiler would do this, or perhaps you might consider a wood-burning stove as part of your step towards self-sufficiency? See the section on Bio-mass later in this chapter.

A solar thermal system takes only around a day to install. It needs very little maintenance and there are virtually no running costs.

The system works by water from the mains heating up as it passes through the solar thermal tubes, then being piped into your hot water tank. In the summer months this means you can heat practically all of your hot water from the solar panel. In winter you will still need to use the boiler but it won't have to work quite as hard as the water is already partly warmed up. On average, therefore, a solar thermal system in your home could provide around 50% of the energy required to deliver hot water, allowing for heat losses from stored water.

Grants
See the Grants section in Harnessing Solar Energy for general information on grants and website details of the government agencies.

ENERGY, WATER AND FUEL

In England, Wales and Northern Ireland the grant for solar thermal systems could be an overall maximum of £400 or 30% of the relevant eligible costs, whichever is the lower – the grant will only be valid for three months, so make sure you have received your grant before you start installation. Grant validity is three months for installations in existing buildings and six months for those under construction.

In Scotland, the grant is currently set at 30% of the installed cost of a renewable measure, up to £4,000.

So what's the catch? I believe it's the Time to Break Even.

Time to Break Even

For the purpose of this calculation I have assumed:

- The inflation rate on fuel and the lost bank interest due to making a large capital investment cancel each other out and have been removed from the calculation.
- Most people will currently being using gas to power their boiler, in which case I have assumed the price of gas to be 2.62p per kilowatt hour (kWh).
- About half the household water heating requirements are catered for by the solar thermal system.

Net cost of a solar thermal system, including: • solar panels or plates • Installation • new cylinder	£3,500
Government grant (maximum)	£400 (England, Wales, Northern Ireland)
VAT at 5% on 3,500	£175
Gross cost, after grant and VAT is applied	Net cost minus grant plus VAT £3,500 – £400 + £175 = £3,275
Annual water heating cost	12 hours/day, 365 days/year, 2.62p/kWh 12 x 365 x £0.0262 = £114.76
Energy provided by solar heating	50%
Annual fuel saving	Energy provided x heating cost 50% x £114.76 = £57.38
Time to Break Even	Gross cost divided by annual fuel saving 3,275 / £57.38 = 57 years

Ground, Air and Water Source Heat Pumps

Reality Check: ȲȲȲ ☺☺☺ £££- ♥

Heat pumps are already familiar in the domestic environment, as they are used in fridges and air conditioners.

Ground source heat pumps take advantage of the year-round constant temperature of 12°C just a few metres below the surface of the earth and transfer this heat into the house to radiators or underfloor heating. The latter is generally preferred, as they tend to operate at lower temperatures. The system comprises:

- a coil of pipe buried in a trench in the garden so that water with antifreeze can be pumped around it, absorbing the heat of the ground
- a pump with compressor and condenser to transfer the heat to a hot water system
- a distribution system such as underfloor heating or radiators; a storage facility may also be used for hot water supply

Costs for a ground source heat pump start at around £7,000.

Similar to ground source heat pumps, you might also want to consider:

- air source heat pumps, which extract the heat from the air, which is then drawn over coils that extract energy
- water source heat pumps, which take heat from the water and convert it into a gas, which is then condensed, releasing heat

Grants
In England, Wales and Northern Ireland, ground source heat pumps are eligible for an overall maximum grant of £1,200 or 30% of the relevant eligible costs, whichever is the lower. Air source heat pumps are eligible for grants up to £900 or 30% of the relevant eligible costs, whichever is the lower. Grant validity is six months for installations in both existing buildings and those under construction.

In Scotland, the grant is currently set at 30% of the installed cost of a renewable measure, up to £4,000.

ENERGY, WATER AND FUEL

Lighting

ⓘ Did you know...? Dirty windows can reduce the amount of light entering a room by up to 20%. Dirt on the windowpanes also affects the quality of the light. Keep your windows sparkling clean – see the Home chapter to make your own cleaner.

Compact Fluorescent Lamps (CFLs)

If you do just one thing: switch to energy-saving light bulbs the next time you need to replace a bulb.

Reality Check: (🕈) (☺) £- ♥

Compact fluorescent lamps (CFLs) are the now readily-available energy-saving bulbs that look a bit like coils – they take a few seconds to get going, but once they've got themselves fully illuminated they're every bit the equal of a conventional bulb. These days it's even possible to get the CFLs in a variety of sizes and shapes. You don't have to have weird loops sticking out of the top of your lampshades any more! There are even some that will work with a dimmer switch.

Energy Saving

ⓘ Did you know...? Energy-saving light bulbs use between a fifth and a quarter of the electricity that standard tungsten-filament bulbs require to do the same job, so swapping to energy-saving CFLs when you next need to replace a light bulb will save you money (and help to do your bit for the environment too).

Standard Bulb	CFL
25 W	6 W
40 W	8–11 W
60 W	13–18 W
100 W	20–25 W

Just changing to one energy-saving light bulb could save you around 4p per day or £14.60 per year. Multiply that by the number of bulbs you have in the house and you're talking a great deal of money. And because the bulb will last up to 10 times longer than a standard bulb, it could save you around £60 before it needs replacing.

HOW TO LIVE ON LESS

You will need to spend more upfront to buy low-energy light bulbs, but they are more cost-effective in the long run as they use less electricity and don't need to be replaced as often.

Time to Break Even

Of all the energy-saving improvements that you can quickly and easily do at home, energy-saving bulbs have one of the fastest payback times:

Energy consumed by tungsten-filament bulb	100 W = 0.1 kW
Energy consumed by CFL bulb	20 W = 0.02 kW
Cost of CFL (without any Discount)	£2.09 = 209p
Hours illuminated per day	5
Electricity price (my most-used tariff)	10.31 per kWh = £0.1031
Cost of use of tungsten-filament bulb per day	Energy consumed times hours illuminated times electricity price 0.1 x 5 x £0.1031 = £0.05155 = 5.16p
Cost of use of CFL bulb per day	Energy consumed times hours illuminated times electricity price 0.02 x 5 x £0.1031 = £0.01031 = 1.03p
Saving per day	Cost of use of tungsten filament minus cost of use of CFL 5.16p – 1.03p = 4.13p
Time to Break Even	Cost of CFL divided by saving per day 209p / 4.13p = 51 days = 1 month 3 weeks

I think the biggest drawback with energy-saving light bulbs is that they contain around 5 mg of mercury – a toxic chemical, very definitely environmentally *unfriendly*. If you break a bulb at home, the advice is to open a window for at least 15 minutes, during which time you should stay out of the room, clear the breakage carefully wearing gloves and put all the broken pieces into a plastic bag, then dispose of this at the council-provided waste-disposal facility. Finished bulbs should similarly be taken to the council waste-disposal facility, rather than being added to the household waste. Supporters of CFLs argue that, since burning coal for electricity is the greater source of mercury pollution, using energy-efficient CFLs will actually reduce the overall amount of mercury emissions, since less coal will be burnt.

ENERGY, WATER AND FUEL

Light-emitting Diodes (LEDs)

ⓘ Did you know...? You can now buy a pocket-sized wind-up LED torch for under £5. Larger and more expensive versions can provide up to 20 hours of continuous light and several brightness settings.

I'm sure you'll already be familiar with light-emitting diodes (LEDs) – they're the little coloured indicator lights on your PC, your video, your car and numerous other electrical goods – but maybe you hadn't realised the same technology is starting to become available for lighting your home. Like their PC counterparts, LEDs for the home come in a range of colours (including white) and sizes. And because they do not generate much heat, they are good for use where you might not otherwise have a lamp, e.g. to illuminate the tread of a stair, or as a night light in a bathroom. LED technology has several claims to fame:

- LEDs will last millions of hours before electrical failure.
- They are highly energy-efficient – comparable to the best CFLs – so again reducing the amount of money you spend.
- LEDs are also totally environmentally friendly – there is no mercury in them, so they are easy to dispose of.

Solar Garden Lights

There is a wide variety of solar-powered garden lights on the market, so you should be able to find a style that fits in with your garden – whether wall-mounted, installed along a path or incorporated into your decking. Solar garden lights start from as little as £10, there are no additional installation costs as you can plug the light into the ground yourself, and the energy they use is free and renewable. Throughout the day the lights absorb solar energy and store it in a battery. Like their solar panel counterparts, solar garden lights need daylight (though not necessarily strong sunlight) to absorb energy. At night, a dusk sensor switches the light on. A number of solar garden lights utilise LED technology. Such lights provide a high level of illumination and will last for many years.

HOW TO LIVE ON LESS

Water

Saving Money by Reducing Domestic Water Usage

Reality Check: (🛠) (🕐) £- ❤

✂ Fitting a water meter could help *Budgeting and Planning* the amount of water you use as well as help you live on less. According to a consumer organisation's *Comparison Website*, the average metered bill in England and Wales is almost 15% cheaper than an un-metered bill. Whether a water meter is right for you depends on your water company and your usage – use a calculator available on the *Comparison Website* to do the calculation and make an assessment yourself, or ask your supplier for advice.

> ⓘ Did you know...? About 95% of water delivered to UK homes goes straight down the drain.

Of the total amount of water we use in the home we typically use it as follows:

30% – flushing the loo
25% – personal washing
15% – washing machine
12% – drinking and preparing food
12% – dishwasher and washing up
6% – garden

Much can be done to reduce the amount of water we use, as well as reusing what we already pay for. Taking our usage list from above in order of priority, here are some ideas to reduce domestic water usage.

Toilet Flush

The easiest way to reduce the amount of water you use with every flush is to add a displacement device. These are generally free from your water company, so just ask for one, particularly if you have an older cistern that could be using as much as 9 litres (2 gallons) of valuable drinking-quality water every time you flush. You could use a brick as the displacement device, so long as it doesn't interfere with the workings of the cistern, but a brick will decompose eventually. There are also some neat plastic bags that hang in the cistern and hold back several pints of water. If you are at a point where you need to install a new loo, why not look at the dual-flush type that can deliver half a flush or a whole one, depending on what you need. I also know several families that operate a no-flush-for-a-wee system among themselves – it's entirely up to you.

Personal Wash

It's a bit of an urban myth that showers use less water than baths – not so if you have a power shower or if you spend as much time in the shower as my husband does! OK, if you don't have a power shower and you are in and out in less than five minutes then you are using less water. Otherwise, it would be better to have a bath – we always share ours, which is a fun way of saving water! Other measures include turning the taps off when you are washing, shaving or brushing your teeth. Put the plug in the sink and add a minimum of water to wash in, and use a tooth mug.

⚒ Make sure you fix leaky taps and loos to ensure you are not wasting water unnecessarily. You could use a local *Community Network* to barter plumbing skills for a service or product you can give in return.

Washing Machine

Make sure you have a full load whenever you can; the half-load cycles use more than half the water and energy of a full load.

Preparing Food

As with personal washing, put a plug in the sink and add water, or use a bowl. If the water has just been used for preparing vegetables, throw the resultant grey water onto the compost heap or use it to water plants in the border.

Dishwasher

Make sure you have a full load whenever you can; the half-load cycles use more than half the water and energy of a full load. Hand washing should be done in a bowl to minimise the amount of water used and heat retained.

Garden

There are numerous ways of reducing the amount of water you use on the garden. Take a look at the following list and implement as many as you can. Avoid digging in hot weather – not only is it exhausting, it will also increase the amount of water lost from the soil from evaporation.

Six of the Best: Practical ideas to reduce the amount of water used in the garden.

- Don't water at all. In my experience, established borders don't need watering unless there is a really tough drought, and even then it's surprising how resilient plants and shrubs can be. If you're planting from new, select plants that are suited to the conditions in your garden or survive better in hot and dry conditions. In my garden the plants have to contend with extremely windy conditions, which quite apart from the battering they are delivered, means they dry very quickly. Nevertheless, now they are mature I generally leave them to their own devices. If you're in a location that gets particularly dry and hot in the summer, choose plenty of drought-tolerant plants – these generally have silvery leaves and are sometimes downy or waxy. Lawns naturally turn brown in a prolonged dry spell but won't have died – they quickly recover when it rains again – so don't be tempted to use the sprinkler. However, if you are establishing a new lawn, whether seed or turf, I do recommend keeping this well watered in the first season.
- Water more effectively. Pour water from a can directly over the root area of each plant in the coolest parts of the day – early morning or late evening – so that most of it does not evaporate. Occasional long soakings encourage roots to go deeper into the soil to seek out water stored in the ground. This is a better strategy than regular light watering, which encourages roots to rise to the surface and makes the plant unstable.
- Improve soil structure. Add a good quantity of organic matter, such as garden compost, to the soil to improve its structure and water-retaining capability and thus the frequency at which watering will be required.
- Reduce evaporation. Try to organise your planting so that there is always a canopy of foliage covering the soil. Where there are gaps, put a layer of mulch, such as bark chips or gravel, over the topsoil and around the plants to slow down evaporation from the soil and to suppress weeds.
- Reuse domestic water. Your plants and shrubs (but not crops that you intend to eat) are good candidates for reused grey water from vegetable preparation, the bath or shower – use a minimum of chemicals or detergents.
- Don't waste water with potted plants. Make sure you are using the largest pot suitable for the plant and add some water-retaining granules to the soil. A watering spike can also be pushed into the soil to release drops of water only when the plant needs moisture.

✗ You can't switch water provider, as the structure of the market prevents choice. Therefore a big decision for your water supply is how you're billed. As with other utility suppliers Direct Debit payment often

ENERGY, WATER AND FUEL

reduces the overall bill and allows you to improve *Budgeting and Planning* by having the same payment every month.

Reusing Domestic Water

Reality Check: (☤) (☺) £- ♥

There are numerous, simple ways to reuse water.

From the Kitchen
Water that has been used to soak, boil or steam vegetables and pulses should not simply be thrown down the sink but used to:

- top up the stock pot (I don't personally like starchy water from soaking or cooking potatoes, pasta or pulses in my stock)
- add to the compost bin
- when cooled, water plants in the border
- while still boiling hot, throw over the weeds coming up between paving slabs on the patio – they really don't like it!

From the Bathroom
So-called "grey water" used in baths, showers and the sink can be reused in the garden so long as you use biodegradable detergents, and then not too much. Use a siphon to move your bath water from the bathroom out to the garden: you can buy primer pumps and hosepipes from the local DIY centre. Once collected, never use grey water on any plant you intend to eat and don't store grey water for more than 24 hours. Do not be tempted to use grey water to fill your water butt – keep this for rainwater harvesting only, as grey water may contaminate it.

Self-sufficiency: Collecting Rainwater

Reality Check: ☤ ☺☺ ££- ♥

> If you do just one thing: install a water butt to collect rainwater for nothing.

I have a huge water butt – it's called a pond but it works on the same principle as a water butt. Rainwater is collected from the whole of the rear roof of the back of the house and piped (underground in our case) to the pond. The pond is home to a host of wildlife that take care of the slugs and snails in the garden and a range of other pests, but I also use it as a source of water supply for the garden. I fill up my watering can from the pond, swish out my kitchen waste collection bowl once I've deposited the contents on the compost heap (and then I throw that water on the compost as well), and occasionally siphon off water for lengthier shrub watering when the drought hits. If I bothered to wash my car, I could also use pond water – those people that know me well know that I never wash my car!

Installing a water butt in your garden is a bit of a no-brainer. Every time you use stored water you save mains water, slow down the water meter and save yourself money. You will have also stopped storm water entering the drainage system. A 190 litres (42 gallon) recycled plastic butt with stand and downpipe connector kit costs from around £45 and is easy to install – you may even find your local authority is offering water butts at a discount specifically to encourage you to have one. Rainwater is then collected from the roof of your house via the downpipes and available totally free of charge for you to use on the garden, to top up bird baths, wash the car, etc. You need to make sure the butt is raised sufficiently to allow you to get your favourite watering can under the tap at the bottom of the butt, that the top is covered so that it keeps the water clean, that it is child- and animal-proof and minimises evaporation, and that an overflow system exists – which could just be another water butt.

> ① Did you know...? There's a neat rain-harvesting system called a Rainpiper that can store enough rainwater for 30 days' garden supply, all in a vertical "rain bank" which is fixed to the side of your house (or garage). It doesn't quite make the tea, but it can water your garden while you're away. See www.clearwell-rainpiper.co.uk.

Storing and Reusing Rainwater

Reality Check: ϒ ϒ ①① £££- ❤

It is possible to store the rain you have collected off the roof and have it diverted back into the house for flushing toilets and potentially using in washing machines – in fact it's an ideal candidate for the latter, as rainwater is particularly soft. A storage tank would be needed, sited where it will be kept free of frost, and a filtration system added to ensure the collected water is free from leaves, moss and other debris. Then you'll need to add a pump in order to get the water from the tank into a dedicated tank (more expense!) in the loft or even straight to the place where you will use it (e.g. to the toilet for flushing). Such a system could cost you as much as £2,500 fully installed, but if you've implemented all the other measures for reducing domestic water usage the savings wouldn't be very exciting – say, around £50 per year. The time to break even would therefore be in the order of 50 years.

Fuel

Saving Money by Spending Less on Fuel

⚒ The *Comparison Website* www.petrolprices.com enables you to find the lowest petrol prices in your area, and includes information from 9,763 petrol stations. You have to register on the site to find out where you can buy the cheapest fuel, but registration is free and means you will get regular updates on changing fuel prices in your area.

⚒ Register with the website www.pipelinecard.org to join the campaign to get between 5p and 7p per litre off fuel. The programme has been set up by a motoring enthusiast who wants to use the clout of a large body of people to lobby and negotiate with fuel retailers to get cheaper petrol.

If you do just one thing: reduce your car fuel consumption by driving efficiently; take a look at the following list and save around £120 a year on your fuel bill.

Reality Check: (Ƴ) (🕐) (£-) ❤

Six of the Best: Practical ideas to reduce your fuel consumption.

- Reduce drag by driving with the windows up (bad news for fresh air freaks like me!), taking off the roof rack/bike carrier if you're not going to use them, and unloading heavy items you don't need for the journey. Even reducing the amount of fuel you have on board will reduce overall weight and thus increase fuel efficiency.
- Keep your car in top condition: a well-tuned engine improves the car's performance and limits fuel consumption. Keep your tyres inflated to the correct pressure: fuel consumption increases if your tyres are under-inflated (and your tyres wear out quicker).
- Keep your speed down. It can cost you up to 25% more in fuel to drive at 70 mph compared to 55 mph. Harsh acceleration and braking can use up to 30% more fuel – it's much more economic to allow the engine to slow you down naturally by deceleration than by using the brake.

- Use the rev counter to guide gear changes – change up before 2,500 rpm (petrol) and 2,000 rpm (diesel).
- Avoid short journeys – a cold engine uses almost twice as much fuel, and catalytic converters can take five miles to become effective – much better to walk or cycle!
- Don't rev the engine or sit for a long time idling – it's more efficient to turn your engine off if you're going to be stuck in a traffic jam for more than a few minutes.

🛠 Fuel *Discount Vouchers* from supermarkets are generally transferable – i.e. they're not bar-coded with your loyalty card – so you can share them between friends and neighbours to get the Timing of your fuel purchase correctly coordinated with an empty tank.

Taking the Idea a Bit Further

If you're keen to take a greater step towards saving on the fuel bill, the following ideas might appeal – obviously they involve some up-front expenditure.

- Consider buying a small, efficient car for your everyday needs and taking the train or renting a larger car for longer journeys when you need it.
- Consider using a hybrid vehicle, which saves energy by using an electric battery as well as petrol.
- Consider converting your car to Liquid Petroleum Gas (LPG) or bio-mass (see later). These fuels are much less polluting than petrol and are becoming increasingly available.

Bio-mass

What is Bio-mass?

Bio-mass is a non-fossil fuel made from living, or recently living, things. It may be plant-, animal- or vegetable-derived material. There are five basic categories of bio-mass base material:

- virgin wood, from forestry, untreated wood products or from wood processing
- energy crops: high-yield crops grown specifically for energy applications like rape, sugar cane and maize
- agricultural residues: residues from agriculture harvesting or processing
- food waste, from food and drink manufacture, preparation and processing, and post-consumer waste – chip fat is a popular choice

ENERGY, WATER AND FUEL

- industrial waste and biodegradable co-products from manufacturing and industrial processes

Bio-mass is considered a renewable energy source because it can be replaced at the same rate at which it is used. Bio-mass can be used to fuel our cars, either in total or in part. In the UK our government has a Renewal Transport Fuel Obligation, which requires fuel companies to add 5% bio-fuel to all petrol and diesel sold on their forecourts by 2010 – and it can be used to heat our living space, typically in the form of wood pellets, wood chips and wood logs.

Using Bio-Mass to Create Bio-Fuel

> ⓘ Did you know...? Under UK law you are allowed to make up to 2,500 litres of bio-fuel a year without having to pay duty or VAT. All you need is a homebrew kit, available for under £1,000, and either new or used cooking oil. The amount of bio-fuel allowed could power a family diesel for up to 40,000 miles.

Back in the early 1990s, my husband and I were privileged to spend a wonderful holiday in Brazil with our friends Ruy and Paula. While we were there, they showed us that a number of cars were running entirely on sugar cane alcohol – there was a strong drive with tax incentives to reduce the country's dependency on imported oil. Until recently, I hadn't given it much more thought, but looking more closely at the biomass market in the UK market to write this chapter, I checked again with Ruy to see whether the experiment in Brazil had been successful.

Ruy told me that the original experiment started well and all the necessary infrastructure was put in place, but although the cars were good, the engines simply didn't last as long as their petrol counterparts. This, combined with the decrease in the price of oil around that time, undermined the cost-effectiveness of alcohol-driven cars, and eventually they stopped being sold. Then, later in the nineties, instead of pure alcohol-driven cars, the government added bio-fuel to normal petrol – much as we are now doing in Britain today. For the last few years, after yet another rise in the price of oil, the Brazilian automobile industry started manufacturing cars that could use alcohol again, but this time the technology had improved, such that dual-fuel engines are supplied. Now in Brazil, a large number of cars that roll off the production line can use either sugar-cane alcohol or petrol – the driver chooses what to put in his car, based on availability and price.

Two types of bio-fuel are currently available on the UK market – bio-diesel and bio-ethanol. Bio-diesel is a combustible fuel derived from crushed rapeseed oil or purified waste vegetable oil. The fuel must be blended with diesel at a proportion not greater than 5% (i.e. 5% bio-diesel and 95% diesel). Bio-ethanol is sugar beet or wheat, fermented and distilled to produce ethanol. When combined with petrol it produces a combustible fuel. The combination used in petrol engines is typically 85% bio-ethanol and 15% petrol; however, at present in the UK there is limited availability of flexible fuel vehicles that are able to run on this blend. Petrol vehicles need converting to be able to run on this fuel.

Using Bio-mass in the Home
Wood-burning Stove

I love the comfort of a roaring open fire – I can sit for hours mesmerised by the flames, enjoying the heat, intoxicated by the scent of burning wood and listening to the crackle and splutter. However, I have spent enough Christmas and New Year holidays in draughty French country gîtes to know also some of the major drawbacks of an open fire: they can be a pain to get started, though once you've done it a few times you learn the knack; the smell of the smoke eventually pervades everything you're wearing and gets into the coats hanging up in the hall; and the amount of space they actually heat is probably only within a couple of metres of the fire itself, which is why you always get the armchairs set either side of the hearth.

My girlfriend Rhoda has the most beautiful Inglenook fireplace, and originally had an open fire in it. She described many of the same drawbacks of an open fire, but also said that she was always frightened of leaving the fire still burning, even at a low ember, when they went to bed because it just didn't feel safe – they often got sparks spitting out into the room and burning small holes in the carpet. Now they have swapped to a stunning black enamel wood-burning stove and have the option of either opening the glass doors to enjoy the fire direct, or closing them to continue to enjoy the heat, but feel totally secure that there will be no fallout. Rhoda also confirms that the heat output by the wood-burning stove is significantly more than the open fire had been – so much so that she has now put a second stove in the dining room.

What I hadn't been able to quantify until now was the heating inefficiency of an open fire, but research has its rewards. According to new statistics, open fires are only around 20–25% efficient. A wood-burning stove, on the other hand, is equally attractive and overcomes all the

ENERGY, WATER AND FUEL

drawbacks of an open fire, as well as being economical to run and environmentally-friendly. A modern wood-burning stove is around 75–90% efficient – that's at least three times more efficient than an open fire, meaning that you only need one-third the amount of wood to generate the same amount of heat. Since the doors of the stove can be open or closed, smoke management is far easier, and they are pretty straightforward to get started with kindling and firelighters.

Rhoda buys unseasoned wood that she gets mainly from the woodman of a local estate, though her husband is also able to get some for nothing through his business. The wood then gets stored in a large garden shed for a year to make sure it's completely dry. Her lounge stove gets lit most evenings during the winter, and the dining-room stove when they are entertaining. However, since the stove only takes a few minutes to get started and less than 15 minutes before the room is lovely and warm, they can more or less put the stove on whenever the room feels a bit chilly.

Although Rhoda's choice of fuel has been unseasoned wood, there are several types of wood fuel used by wood-burning stoves – check before you buy what your stove will use:

Logs or Other Wood
Any untreated wood is good fuel for a wood-burning stove, and you should be able to forage for free wood in your neighbourhood. Untreated wood pallets are available from various trades. Household waste wood (which would otherwise end up in a landfill) is fine, so long as it's not painted or treated timber. And, of course, the wood should be well seasoned. When wood is fully dry the bark comes off easily, and two logs banged together ring like a bell – unseasoned wood makes a dull thud.

Wood Chips
Wood-chip burners have the advantage that they use a more homogenous fuel type, and can therefore be automated to control temperature settings.

Wood Pellet
Wood pellets are the densest form of wood fuel and are typically compressed sawdust. Their relatively small size enables the right quantity of fuel to be readily and accurately fed into the boiler and, like wood-chip burners, temperature settings can be controlled.

Wood Fuel Briquettes

Wood fuel briquettes are a reconstituted fuel, similar to pellets but comparable to log fuel in size. However, their size means that they must be burnt on the same appliances and installation systems as logs, but having a generally slower burning time, they are more suited to "idling" conditions.

All the ash produced by the wood-burning stove can be added to the compost heap. However, the stoves do not need to be cleared of their ash every day as an open fire would – in fact, a bed of ash in a wood-burning stove will help the wood to burn.

Connecting the Wood-burning Stove to Other Systems

Depending on how frequently you will use your wood-burning stove, you might additionally consider connecting it to other household systems, for example:

- integral back boiler
- radiators
- underfloor heating

Both Rhoda's stoves are stand-alone and don't connect to any other systems. She does use the flat tops to keep dishes warm that she's serving for dinner, as well as the coffee pot to provide us with a good strong coffee to drink with our after-dinner brandy.

Cost

There is a wide range of wood-burning stoves on the market, and you can choose from traditional black cast iron to something ultra-modern with a steel or ceramic finish. Prices start from about £500, but you should assume a start price of £2,000 when full installation is taken into account.

Grants

In England, Wales and Northern Ireland, grants are available for:

- automated wood-pellet-fed room heaters/stoves: overall maximum of £600 or 20% of the relevant eligible costs, whichever is the lower
- wood-fuelled boiler systems: overall maximum of £1,500 or 30% of the relevant eligible costs, whichever is the lower

Grant validity periods for both technologies are six months for both installations in existing buildings and those under construction.

chapter 3

Home and Leisure

Purchasing products and services for home and leisure lends itself to a broad range of techniques from the toolkit. There are simply hordes of ways to live on less without compromising your quality of life. I would almost go as far as saying that you shouldn't ever have to pay full price for anything you want to buy within this category.

Going down the self-sufficiency route to take care of your home needs generally requires drawing on your latent skills and talents to make your own products, although I've included a number of home-made cleaning products and natural cosmetics that are simple and easy to prepare.

Also included in this chapter are some ideas for potentially earning additional income – by sweating your home assets, trading your skills and selling excess items.

House and Home

Reality Check: ♈ ☯☯ (£-)

✼ Not everyone will have a mortgage, but most of us will have home and contents insurance and many of us life insurance. As with energy suppliers in the last chapter, the plethora of deals offered by mortgage dealers and insurance brokers are now very easy to search, compare and purchase online, either through a *Comparison Website* – a very good way to get started at least – or direct with the preferred company. Several companies are now bundling insurance deals if you go direct or take out more than one type of policy with them – it's their answer to the increasing strength of the comparison websites, and avoids you having to pay commission to the middle-man. If it's time for you to change your mortgage or insurance, I urge you to try these sites – most people I know that have used them have been able to save a significant amount of money by changing supplier.

The last time we needed to change our mortgage, we did some background research using the *Comparison Websites* and numerous financial articles both in the national press and online, but then returned to a mortgage broker (i.e. a human being!) that we had successfully used in the past to help us find the right deal for our needs. Mortgage broker services are free, since they get commission from the supplier not the client, and they have a very detailed knowledge of the market. Our existing mortgage lender turned out not to be the cheapest, so we had intended to change supplier. However, the broker suggested we give our original lender the opportunity to better their offer, on the basis that we were about to stop doing business with them in favour of a competitor. The lender was very keen to keep us as a customer, and offered us an improved rate that obviated the need to change.

⚒ Since many of the items you will purchase for the home involve sizeable expenditure – furniture, white goods, carpets, computer, TV equipment, etc. – this is a good opportunity to investigate whether the supplier and product you want is available through a *Cash Back Portal.* Like window-shopping, it costs nothing to browse…

> ⓘ Did you know…? In late 2008 a budding media entrepreneur was masterminding a multi-million pound plan to provide a virtual reality online shopping experience complete with a range of graphics, animations and imagery. The experience would duplicate real-life shopping, whereby you would "visit" high street shops, see the products stacked on shelves, and invite your friends from your *Social Network* to join you. The online high street would be free from pickpockets and beggars but would have a link to the meteorological office so that you would "experience" the correct weather for the day.

⚒ Every store has a Sale – it means you may have to wait to make your purchase but it will be worth the wait. We've all seen the TV advertisements for the furniture shops that are having yet another sale,

HOME AND LEISURE

seemingly without any time between the current one and the last one. But all shops do have a normal sales cycle and for the most part they are predictable. Gone are the days of simply the "January Sales". Now there are sales before and during most of the major public holiday, end-of-season clearances, and one-off events giving a percentage discount off everything. Sales assistants may not be able to confirm whether your desired purchase will appear in the next sale, but they should be able to tell you when the event takes place.

✻ Hand-in-hand with the sale, you may also find your supplier offers extended *Credit* terms such as interest-free credit for a fixed number of years and nothing to pay for an initial period. This can be an excellent *Budgeting and Planning* mechanism to spread the cost of major purchases over time.

We've just completed installation of an en-suite bathroom – it's taken a year from start to finish, but this was because we purchased the tiles, suite and furnishings over an extended period, taking advantage of several suppliers' spring, summer and end-of-line *Sales*. The main company we used did not feature in a *Cashback Portal*, but if it had, we could have earned ourselves some additional money. As it happens, had we owned shares in the supplier we would have got a discount of around £500…potentially worthwhile if you are a regular stock-market trader and wish to invest temporarily in the supplier of your chosen goods.

Travel

Reality Check: ⟁ ◎ £-

✻ Just about all forms of travel can be searched, compared, reserved and purchased through an *Online Shopping* website. Advance rail tickets are often significantly discounted, so if you get the Timing right by *Budgeting and Planning* well in advance, you should be able to fund your trip more economically. Several fares only last for a short period – you need to get to know how the different companies set their tariffs – and typically the more restricted the fare (time of day, day of the week, number of en route changes, forfeiting the right to change your itinerary), the cheaper the ticket.

For my recent birthday treat, Ian bought a weekend at the Eden Project, inclusive of a hotel for the weekend and first-class rail travel from home

HOW TO LIVE ON LESS

to St. Austell. The usual first-class return fare is around £300 for two tickets from our local station; Ian paid £83 because he was able to book well in advance.

✂ Conversely, numerous *Online Shopping* websites offer improved deals, particularly on airline flights (though typically not using budget airlines) if you wait right until the last minute. This is because a consolidator is looking to fill the final seats on a flight. The drawback is you may not get a flight to a planned destination, thus making it difficult to decide a long way in advance where you want to go – but if you like to live life on the edge and not know where you are going until a few days before, then you can pick up a very good deal indeed.

In recent years, Ian and I have successfully used budget airline websites to advance book flights for weekends and longer holidays, taking advantage of "1p per flight" offers. We have now been to Berlin, Prague and the south of France for 1p each way (which results in a total of around £35 when tax and luggage are added), because we were able to book several months out. Coupled with a good deal on hotels (through *Loyalty Cards* and *Timing*), we have managed several successful European holidays on quite a restricted budget. In addition, we have judiciously saved *Loyalty Card* points to exchange for Air Miles to fund long-haul flights and associated accommodation.

✂ All rail networks and operators are obliged by their franchise agreements to offer you Discount cards. If you are a young person, in full-time education, part of a family group or a senior citizen, you should be eligible for a railcard. Railcards cost £24 for one year, and several are available for £65 for three years. Associated with all railcards is a range of discounts on leisure activities, restaurants, hotels, cinemas, etc. around the country. For full details of railcards and leisure offers, see www.nationalrail.co.uk. Terms and conditions apply; some restrictions apply for travelling before 10 am and/or when journeys are made wholly within London and the Southeast area. If you are a senior citizen, check with your local council – some actually pay for you to have a senior railcard!

✂ Bus and coach fares also offer good opportunities to make savings. Following on from the introduction of railcards, bus and coach operators soon jumped on the bandwagon and started to offer a wide range of special *Discounts*. Check with your operator for details.

HOME AND LEISURE

Holidays

Reality Check: ⚥ ① £

> ① Did you know...? The neighbouring towns of Copenhagen (Denmark) and Malmo (Sweden) have now boarded the BOGOF (buy-one-get-one-free) gravy train by having a marketing campaign for "One Destination – Two Countries". Since the Oresund Bridge was completed joining the two towns, the tourist boards are encouraging holidaymakers to fly to one destination and get the other thrown in for free!

As a couple we aim to take the following:

- at least one sailing holiday per year – could be one week or two, definitely somewhere warm like the Mediterranean or the Caribbean, or occasionally further afield
- what I would call a "proper" holiday (i.e. where you get to hang your clothes up in a wardrobe and sleep in a real bed – not like on a yacht) – could be anywhere in the world, but we are great fans of Europe
- several weekend breaks – UK, Europe, visiting friends, possibly another sailing jaunt
- Christmas shopping weekend in a new city, at home or abroad – we find it gives us more inspiration (not to mention focus) than going to the local high-street stores

All this means we need to be careful how we fund our holidays so as not to blow the budget and we have become experts in finding *Online Shopping* deals, using *Discount Vouchers*, taking advantage of opportunities offered through *Loyalty Cards*. Most of the major sailing companies offer discounts through their websites and during the Boat Show, plus we use a "last-minute" sailing website called Latesail. I accept that sailing may not be your activity holiday of choice, but I use our experience to illustrate the fact that, whatever you choose to do, you should be able to find a way to fund your holiday at a lot less than the full price. My husband also enters various competitions that might afford us a "free" trip: one year it paid off and we won a holiday worth £2,000 – we had a magnificent fortnight in Corsica!

As you may have gathered, we tend to build and book our holidays ourselves, selecting flights, hotels, yachts and car hire online, either direct or through an *Air Miles Portal*, then organising rail, taxi, boat and bicycle trips when we arrive. However, package holidays can also be an extremely cost-effective way of taking a holiday, particularly if booked at the last minute. If you're not too fussy where you go, and are prepared to travel at unsociable hours, you can pick up some real bargains within a week or two of your travel dates. Numerous holiday companies have *Online Shopping* websites that are available to search and select.

Days Out

Reality Check: Ƴ ⌚ £-

⚒ You'll see in the Travel section (above) the numerous *Discounts* available if you own a railcard of some description. Independent of these, *Loyalty Card* points are also tradable for a wide range of days out.

⚒ If you are a member of The National Trust (see www.nationaltrust.org.uk) then entry and parking is free to over 300 historic houses and gardens, plus parking at countryside and coastal locations. The cost of membership varies according to whether you are an individual, family or senior citizen and whether you choose annual or life membership, and this is a good example of where paying by *Direct Debit* attracts a very good discount – 25% on all annual membership fees.

⚒ Register (for free) with the *Online Shopping* website www.familydayoutuk.co.uk and you'll get sent a report to your e-mail address that identifies 50 free days out and numerous discounts within the UK (or 250 free days out if you are prepared to become a "Gold" member at a cost of £6.99 per year, which additionally includes visitor guides and videos, discounts, and access to numerous events).

Don't forget also the wide range of completely free local attractions, including museums and galleries, visiting old churches and cathedrals, open farms, walking on the beach or in the woods, cycling to the nearest park for a home-made picnic...the possibilities are endless.

⚒ Children, students, senior citizens, families of four and job seekers all qualify for *Discounts* at local cinemas. In addition, some cinemas offer a monthly membership card that gives you unlimited entrance to movies – any day, any time – for a very reasonable amount. Further, some cinemas offer an "early bird" *Discount* for movies screened before a particular time, generally around 5 pm.

HOME AND LEISURE

✄ A useful ticket-swap website is www.scarletmist.com. This site introduces buyers and sellers to each other (rather than specifically selling anything itself). Tickets for theatre, concerts and a range of events are available here at face value or less.

Fitness

Reality Check: ⚥ ⏱ £-

✄ If you are planning to join a gym, my advice is not to do so until after the New Year rush or straight after the summer holidays. Get the *Timing* right and it could save you money in joining fees or even the monthly subscription, as people join gyms when they become aware of their recent excesses – this is when gym membership peaks and it may be more difficult to negotiate a good deal. Wait until the rush dies down, then shop around the gyms in your area to find what suits you best. In our area we also have a new "budget" gym that has all the facilities you could wish for, but at a fraction of the price of some of the national chains.

If you prefer to "go it alone" on the exercise front, there are of course numerous activities that you can do effectively for free, but which will require an initial outlay to purchase the right equipment, clothing or footwear if you don't already have them. Examples include indoor or outdoor cycling, running and walking. Other activities like yoga or simple aerobics can be undertaken at home if you purchase a DVD that will guide you through the postures and exercises. I always find exercising with someone else is more fun and motivational than being completely alone – and it means you'll be encouraged to keep to a routine rather than ducking out at the last minute.

✄ Second-hand (often unused) exercise equipment is a popular offer on Internet *Auction* or *Community Network* sites, as many people purchase the equipment with good intentions, but never get around to actually using it, or at least not as frequently as they anticipated. Treadmills, exercise bikes, heart-rate monitors, dumbbells, cross-trainers, fitness balls, etc. should all be available at a good price.

HOW TO LIVE ON LESS

Smaller Items: Clothes, Books, Music

✂ If you need an outfit for a particular occasion and don't want to buy a new one or (God forbid!) wear something you've worn before, why not hire an outfit for the night? You should be able to rent both formal and informal wear for around £50–£100. It'll be cheaper than buying something new that may only get worn a few times, plus you could wear something new every time you go to an important function.

✂ To accompany your new look, why not get a wash-and-blow-dry (or even a cut if you are confident) at a hairdressing salon that needs models to train their staff: you will get your hair done for free, and the apprentice gets the chance to use a real head of hair rather than a mannequin.

✂ *Budget Clothing Shops* are a great source of fashionable and affordable clothing – don't expect to be able to purchase classical or long-lasting clothes. *Charity Shops* also have very affordable second-hand clothing, though perhaps you may not be able to get something at the height of fashion.

✂ Swapping – give as well as receive. We already have an informal book swap at our gym – someone is always returning a book to a friend, who then offers it up to anyone else who wants to read it. This is generally accompanied by the quick five-minute critique of the book (loved it; hated it; couldn't get into that one; have you got the sequel? etc.). But there's no reason to stop at books. It's also easy to swap or loan CDs, costume jewellery, even shoes and clothes among friends, if you just want to have a change from the norm.

Generally when I go on one of my girlie weeks or weekends away, we always end up swapping clothes and jewellery. Usually one of my friends has a "better" cardigan or necklace that complements my outfit, which they are more than pleased to loan for the evening, and it often comes with an invitation to borrow the item in the future.

✂ While books are often good value these days, particularly with a *Multi-Purchase Deal*, don't forget that you can use the local *Library* for free. As well as borrowing numerous books – both fiction and non-fiction – you can also use the reference section for research, or simply to sit and browse through some interesting books that you wouldn't otherwise buy.

HOME AND LEISURE

✻ If you have a PC and broadband connection, why not access the numerous music Online Shopping websites to purchase individual songs or albums that can then be stored and played either on your PC or further downloaded to an MP3 Player. Most sites offer a short clip of the music so that you can listen to the selection before you purchase – very useful if you just want a few individual tunes from an album.

Computer and Communications

> ⓘ Did you know...? Many of the companies that advertise 0870 telephone numbers, and thus charge you a premium rate (and take a share of the cost), also have standard UK telephone lines. Many of them offer an "international" number (advertised with the UK country code prefix +44) for callers from outside the UK to use, but there's no reason why you shouldn't use it too as it's just a standard UK number. Just replace the +44 with a 0. Alternatively, if no "international" number is provided, check out the website www.saynoto0870.com to see if an alternative UK landline number is registered to the subscriber.

✻ Free software. There is a range of non-profit software known as "open source" that is available to download from an *Online Shopping* website for nothing. You should be able to find a package for each of the major activities you want – word processing, financial management, anti-virus and firewall, digital photo editing, etc. See www.download.com, www.freewarefiles.com.

✻ If you and your family or friends each have a PC and broadband connection, then registering with a voice-over-Internet-protocol (VOIP) service like Skype would enable you to make phone calls totally free over the *Internet*. Registration is free of charge but you will need a headset or a phone with a USB plug. Once registered, all calls to other VOIP users are free, and any calls to the outside (i.e. off the Internet) are charged at local rate. See www.skype.com.

✻ Similarly, why not reuse your PC and broadband for social networking – a very effective mechanism for keeping in touch with your loved ones for nothing. Let people know that you are thinking of them on a regular basis by sharing photos, chatting online, sending messages and amusing icons, giving virtual hugs and electronic cards, not to mention playing the wealth of simple games – but watch out...it can be addictive! See www.myspace.com and www.facebook.co.uk.

HOW TO LIVE ON LESS

ⓘ Did you know...? In 2008 more UK Internet users chose to spend time on Christmas Day afternoon accessing their social network rather than listening to the Queen's speech. Activity started to rise from 2 pm, peaking at 5 pm – clearly many people preferring to contact their friends and family rather than listen to the pre-recording of our monarch.

Incremental Income

Six of the Best: Ways of getting a bit more income.

- **Take on extra work:** Earn money (or even Air Miles...hurrah!) by taking part in surveys and market research (see www.whichsurveys.com or www.valuedopinions.co.uk). Review music (www.slicethepie.com). Work as a film extra (www.universalextras.co.uk). Become a mystery shopper (www.retaileyes.co.uk). Take part in psychological or other medical tests (www.entertrials.co.uk).
- **Sell your skills:** Coach others (e.g. in a musical instrument, a foreign language or whatever your strength is) or provide a service (e.g. gardening, dressmaking, dog walking). Home sitting, often combined with pet sitting and simple gardening duties, is becoming more popular while people are on holiday – it can pay you some incremental income, and means the family don't have to spend quite so much on catteries and kennels, plus they have peace of mind that their home is being looked after while they are away.
- **Sweat your assets.** Your home is probably your biggest asset and the major expense – so why not find a way to make it earn its keep? For example: provide your home for a film location; share your garden with someone who wants to grow their own fruit and veg, but doesn't have the space; become a host family for an international student – you get paid to take them in and feed them as part of the family – or take in a lodger. Under the government's Rent a Room scheme, you can earn up to £4,250 a year – around £350 a month – from rental income before you have to pay tax. To qualify for Rent a Room tax relief, the property must be your main home and the room must be furnished. Any rent you get above £4,250 will be taxed at 20% if you pay tax at the basic rate or at 40% if you are a higher-rate taxpayer. To advertise your available room and find lodgers/flatmates, see www.easyroommate.com.
- **Sell unwanted items:**
  - Our homes, particular the garage or the attic, can often hoard items we no longer need or have room for, yet for some reason we hang on to for ever (and even pack and move them to our next home!). Just as taking control of your finances can be cathartic, de-cluttering the home and dealing with the wealth of unwanted goods that have been collecting dust for some

HOME AND LEISURE

time can be quite liberating, and you may be surprised at how much you can earn by selling them. There are numerous online and physical Auctions or Car Boot Sales that you can use. Pitches for car boot sales tend to cost between £5 and £20, and you can find sales in your area at www.carbootjunction.com.

- There are a number of Online Shopping websites that will take your old or unwanted mobile phone and give you cash – anything from a few pounds up to around £75, depending on the model and the phone's general state of repair. Some provide free postage and packing, others give more in Vouchers than they do in Cash, and some give a donation to charity every time a phone is recycled. See www.love2recycle.com, www.mopay.co.uk, www.envirofone.com. I tried out the websites with a view to selling my antediluvian Nokia 3310 and got the following results:
    - offer of 24p
    - offer of £1.50 or £2 of M&S vouchers
    - offer of £2

It clearly pays, therefore, to check out several sites before you fix on one.

Similarly, old CDs/DVDs/games can be turned into Cash if you use the website www.musicmagpie.co.uk. The site uses Freepost to get your items to them. I tried out the site with two of my old DVDs, with the following results:
- A Scanner Darkly (2006) – valued at 30p
- Girl with a Pearl Earring (2004) – valued at 43p

Maybe not the most exciting amount for just a couple of DVDs, but if you have a large amount to offload (and some better titles than mine!) you could earn a reasonable amount.

- **Get your finances in order** – and claim what is rightfully yours:
    - Make sure you are using an interest-earning bank account, a 0% finance credit card, and the lowest possible mortgage.
    - If you have savings, make sure you are using all the tax-efficient mechanisms you can, e.g. use your ISA allowance – you won't pay tax on the interest accrued as with regular accounts – and invest in tax-free Premium Bonds.
    - Claim all the tax credits you are entitled to, whether it be child benefit, working tax credit, child tax credit – visit www.entitledto.co.uk.
    - Apparently 1 in 3 UK taxpayers are due a refund – check out if you are due a refund at www.refundsdirect.co.uk (which operates on a "no win no fee" basis).
- **If you are a student** (in full- or part-time higher education, or doing a postgraduate course) whose financial problems are getting in the way of studies, check with Access to Learning Funds (ALF) to see if you can be given additional income to support you. See www.direct.gov.uk/en/EducationAndLearning/UniversityAndHigher Education/StudentFinance/FinanceForNewStudents/DG_069884

Self-sufficiency Around the Home

Natural Cleaning Products From Your Store Cupboard

Reality Check: ♈ ☉ £- ♥

Vinegar and Brown Paper....

I've often been intrigued by the line in the Jack and Jill nursery rhyme that says he went to bed to mend his head with vinegar and brown paper. So some time ago I decided to do some research and got completely waylaid by much more interesting articles on the uses for vinegar, and a few other store cupboard staples, for cleaning your home. I've been worried for some time about the viciousness of some of the chemicals in the cleaning products on the market (I'm convinced I'm at less risk from the germs than I am from the cleaning product!), and the number of different bottles I seem to buy, not to mention what effect the chemicals may be having on my sewer (especially as we don't have mains drainage). And thank goodness I don't have small children around the home – I hate to think what harm they could come to if they ever got hold of some of the commercial products!

Much simpler ingredients can be used for many cleaning jobs around the home, at a fraction of the price of the harmful chemical-cocktail commercial cleaners, and most of us have them sitting in the store cupboard. There are many everyday products you can use, and endless recipes, but I'm going to focus on just three ingredients: bicarbonate of soda, lemon juice and vinegar.

Product	Properties	Notes
Bicarbonate of Soda (or baking powder)	A mild abrasive Safe enough to drink Eliminates odour Softens water	Baking powder is bicarbonate of soda mixed with cream of tartar, and works just as well as the pure product.
Lemon Juice	Anti-bacterial Bleaches Cleans Cuts through grease Deodorises Disinfects	This has similar properties to vinegar (see below), but the actual lemon is a useful cleaning tool in its own right.

HOME AND LEISURE

| Vinegar | Cleans
Cuts through grease
Disinfects
Discourages mould
Stain remover | White distilled vinegar is best (and cheapest); white wine vinegar a more expensive substitute. Don't use malt vinegar – it has a pungent aroma which will make your home smell like a fish-and-chip shop, plus it has colour. |

Where and How to Use Natural Cleaning Products

All Around the Home
- To get rid of nasty niffs, mix 8 tbsp bicarbonate of soda with lemon juice, or 3 drops of your favourite essential oil, and place in a pretty bowl or a vase – so much better for asthma sufferers like myself than those squirty shop-bought "air fresheners".
- Wash windows with a solution of 2–3 tbsp vinegar and 3 litres warm water. Dry with crumpled newspaper. Don't clean windows if the sun is on them, or if they are warm, as streaks will show on drying.
- If your kids have drawn on painted surfaces, baking soda applied to a damp sponge can be gently rubbed over the surface, then wiped and rinsed.
- Wallpaper remover: mix equal parts white vinegar and hot water, and apply with a sponge over the old wallpaper to soften the adhesive.

Bathroom
Loo
- Flush the loo then pour undiluted vinegar under the rim to get rid of rings.
- Put 8 tbsp bicarbonate of soda in the bowl and leave overnight.

Bath and Shower
- Mix 100 ml ($3^1/_2$ fl oz) vinegar and 50 ml (2 fl oz) baking soda with 2 litres ($3^1/_2$ pints) water. Use to remove water deposit stains on shower panels, bathroom chrome fixtures, windows, bathroom mirrors, etc.
- Get rid of the body oil and soap scum ring around the bath with a thick paste of two parts bicarbonate of soda to one part vinegar or lemon juice. Apply with a damp cloth; leave for 15 minutes, then rub with a brush or sponge.

HOW TO LIVE ON LESS

Kitchen
- Place a box of bicarbonate of soda anywhere you want to get rid of odours, e.g. next to the kitchen bin, in the fridge, in the freezer.
- Apply baking soda directly with a damp sponge to use as a scourer, or mix it with water and a tiny squirt of washing-up liquid to act as a disinfectant and mild abrasive that can remove hardened dirt and grease.
- To clean the floor, mix together 50 ml (2 fl oz) liquid soap and 100–200 ml (3–7 fl oz) vinegar. If you want to improve the fragrance, add one cup of strong, freshly brewed herbal tea of your choice.
- Stainless steel surfaces can be made clean and shiny with a paste of bicarbonate of soda and water. Apply liberally with a damp cloth. Leave for about five minutes, then wipe.
- Clean a microwave with a cloth dampened in equal parts vinegar and water. To remove microwave odours generally, place some lemon slices in a bowl of water and nuke for a few minutes.
- Cut a lemon in half, sprinkle bicarbonate of soda (or baking powder) onto the cut section, and use to scrub dishes, surfaces, and stains.
- Rub a slice of lemon across a chopping block to disinfect the surface. For tougher stains, squeeze some of the lemon juice onto the spot and let it sit for ten minutes, then wipe.
- Coffee and tea stains in cups can be removed by applying vinegar to a sponge and wiping.

Lounge
- Make a furniture polish by mixing one part olive oil with one part lemon juice. Rub on with a cloth or apply with a spray bottle, then polish with a dry cloth.
- Carpet stains: Mix equal parts white vinegar and water in a spray bottle. Spray directly onto the stain; let it sit for several minutes, then clean with a brush or sponge using warm, soapy water.
- For a more heavy-duty carpet cleaner, mix together 25 g (1 oz) each of salt, borax and vinegar. Rub the paste into the carpet and leave for a few hours. Vacuum when dry.

Laundry
- Add 100 ml (3½ fl oz) of vinegar to the rinse cycle in place of store bought fabric softener – great for anyone with skin allergies, and has the added benefit of breaking down laundry detergent more effectively.
- Bicarbonate of soda softens water, so assists your other cleaners (including laundry detergents) to clean and rinse off more effectively.

HOME AND LEISURE

Outside

- Put one part soda, followed by four parts hot vinegar, down the drain. Leave overnight if possible.
- For small oil and grease spills on the garage floor, throw over some baking soda and then scrub with a wet brush.

Reduce – Reuse – Recycle

Reality Check: (♈) (☺) (£-) ♥

Packaging

> ⓘ Did you know…? The average Briton throws out four times their body weight in rubbish every year, and the vast majority of that is due to packaging.

I hate packaging. Apart from the fact I struggle to open boxes, polythene wrappers and some plastic bottles, I'm always left with a huge pile of rubbish that needs to be dealt with. Luckily, there are now numerous collections from home, and both the council and the local supermarkets are doing a great job providing recycling centres, but I still seem to end up with so much waste. In my area we get fortnightly collections of general rubbish, with the fortnights in between for collections of kitchen and garden waste, cardboard, newspapers, tin cans and bottles. Plastic containers and cartons get taken to the local supermarket (who reward me with "green points"), and the rest, well, that seems to get stored in the garage, the attic, wherever it can be put out of the way before it can be disposed of as a job lot. You know the sort of thing: packaging from the new PC or coffee machine that you're keeping "just in case"; sturdy wine boxes that are just right for carrying six bottles, but somehow you keep forgetting to take shopping with you; refillable detergent containers awaiting a refill…

In recent months I have therefore been trying to reduce the amount of packaging that is brought home. I've got the jute bags for my shopping so that I don't have to have endless plastic bags that split before you get home. In fact, I much prefer the jute bags because they have a flat bottom so that cartons and bottles stand up nicely rather than fall over the vegetables. I've also been buying fruit and vegetables without an extra plastic bag to hold them in and have not had any problem – they just wobble along the conveyer belt and the checkout assistant gathers them up again to weigh and price. At the other end I tip them out into my vegetable rack none the worse for their lack of packaging. Larger items are more problematic, and so far I have refused to compromise on what I want to avoid the packaging, nor have I unpacked the goods and left the packaging in the shop for the retailer to deal with – it's tempting, though!

Leftover Food

> ⓘ Did you know…? About 30% of the food we buy in the UK ends up in the bin.

Waste. Another bugbear of mine. Not just food – though that makes me mad enough – but other things like once-used items that seemed a good idea at the time, or items like PCs and mobile phones that are quickly superseded by faster, smaller, thinner models with ten times more facilities than we are ever likely to use.

I was brought up in a household where leftover food meant tomorrow's meal. My mum often made a curry on a Monday night to use up the Sunday roast (she only ever cooked the amount of vegetables that we would eat at each meal – then strictly saw to it that we actually ate them!), which was combined with a tin of vegetable soup and "curry powder". By far the best meal of the week!

A recent TV programme, however, brought home to me that many people throw out large amounts of food. One programme showed most of a roast chicken being discarded because the family didn't like to touch the carcass to take the meat off the bones! Unbelievable! (If you don't like touching the carcass, don't buy one – just buy the number of breasts you need.) So I took a straw poll of the ladies I meet down the local gym, and everyone seemed to use their leftover food, citing their favourite recipes and just how many ways you can disguise vegetables in pasta sauces to make sure their children ate enough. Why then, if my friends and I all seem to be reusing our leftovers, is so much food being wasted? Is it a lack of cooking skill brought on by the fast food and convenience food world? Or is it lack of shopping discipline that makes us buy more than we actually need for the week?

HOME AND LEISURE

Unwanted Goods

Six of the Best: Practical ideas to reduce, reuse or recycle unwanted goods.

- PC equipment. The RSPB, like many organisations, runs a recycling facility to encourage recycling of mobile phones and inkjet cartridges so that they don't end up in landfill sites – see www.rspb.org.uk/supporting/green/mobile.asp. PCs can be donated to organisations such as www.computeraid.org.uk or www.donateapc.org.uk. Inkjet cartridges may be recycled rather than discarded – just check the packaging to find out your manufacturer's recycling arrangements. All those free CDs that come with magazines and the weekend newspapers make useful scarecrows if strung across vulnerable seedlings, or they can be sprayed or painted to make interesting mobiles for children or Christmas decorations.
- Newspapers can be shredded for the compost, or soaked in water then laid under grass cuttings to act as an effective ground cover to suppress weeds, or made into papier maché for modelling.
- Junk mail and unsolicited marketing phone calls can both be reduced quite successfully by registering with the Mailing Preference Service (www.mpsonline.org.uk) and the Telephone Preference Service (www.tpsonline.org.uk).
- Whether junk or legitimate mail, envelopes can easily be reused if you open them carefully – use large stickers over the address and re-seal the flap.
- Christmas and other greetings cards can be reused to make pretty gift tags or placed in dedicated recycling bins in a number of supermarkets, particularly straight after Christmas.
- Just about any container can be reused either around the home or in the garden to host a variety of fillers. Glass and ceramics can be filled with wax to make candles or pot pourri to fragrance a room. Plastic bottles that are not going to be refilled make useful cloches over seedlings. Any reasonably-sized waterproof container could be used to grow some vegetables, a mini herb garden or a strawberry plant.

Natural, Home-made Cosmetics

Reality Check: ♈ ☺ £- ♥

Like commercial household cleaning products, it's sometimes difficult to know what goes into the manufacture of oils and creams that we put on our skin, through our hair or into our bath. I know one of the main ingredients in many cosmetics is called "acqua" – why don't they just call it water? That's all it is! And as for the rest of the ingredients, some exist simply to ensure incompatible ingredients like oil and water stay held together, and others to prolong shelf life – not exactly doing anything beneficial for our skin. Also, using harsh cosmetics on sensitive skin may be a contributing factor to the increase of eczema and other skin complaints, particularly among children.

When your skin looks good, you radiate health and vitality. But our skin is complex and it takes skill to get the moisture balance right to provide the desired suppleness, softness and evenness. Skin renews itself quickly and efficiently and responds well to treatment. Simple products based on natural oils, whether plant- or animal-based, combined with natural scents and oils from herbs and flowers, can provide us with skin products that do the same job, cost a fraction of the price, and will not irritate or clog our skin as their commercial cousins can.

And, of course, the best skin regime comes from a lifestyle based on drinking plenty of water, eating lots of fresh fruit and vegetables and getting plenty of fresh air, some moderate exercise and a good night's sleep. Try to avoid all those things that you know will make your face look tired, wrinkled and sallow: caffeine, smoking, junk food, alcohol, pollution, endless hours in front of the PC, stress and anxiety.

> ⓘ **Did you know...?** The hops used in beer are soporific and will help you sleep. Rather than drinking beer, use the flowers to make a hop pillow to keep under your normal pillow. If you don't like their distinctive aroma, add more aromatic herbs like chamomile, lemon verbena, rosemary or lavender.

Head-to-Toe Natural Cosmetics

I'm sure there are a number of cosmetics that you feel you can't possibly do without, whether it be a favourite lip-gloss, that expensive, indulgent eye cream, or a rich, scented bath oil that makes you smooth and slithery all over. However, there are numerous home-made preparations that are equally good, and some better – preparations that are exciting to use and will save you money on chemically-charged commercial cosmetics. You can always keep your favourite shop-bought products as the occasional luxury or treat. I've tried out a number of these preparations – particularly those for oily skin, fair hair, tired eyes and feet – and can confirm that they really are effective.

HOME AND LEISURE

Hair
Shampoo

Egg yolk shampoo: Beat two egg yolks into a cup of warm water; massage gently into the scalp then leave for ten minutes before rinsing off.

Egg and herb shampoo:

For light hair:	Make a strong infusion of chamomile or elder flowers.
For dark hair:	Make a strong infusion of rosemary or sage leaves.
For normal and greasy hair:	Add a beaten egg white to the herbal infusion.
For dry hair:	Add a beaten egg yolk to the herbal infusion.

Rinse

If you can stand it, use cold water as your final rinse (or as cool as you can manage).

For light hair:	Add the juice of half a lemon to cold (cool) water.
For dark hair:	Add a little vinegar to cold (cool) water.
To add sheen:	Boil parsley or stinging nettles in water for 20 minutes; cool, strain.
To add lustre:	Pour boiling water over rosemary and steep for half an hour; cool, strain.
To add body:	Boil nettles or fennel leaves in water for 20 minutes; cool, strain.
To draw out light tones:	Boil chamomile flowers in water for 30 minutes; cool, strain.
To lighten hair:	Simmer 4 tbsp ground rhubarb root in 600 ml (1 pint) water for 30 minutes; steep for several hours; cool, strain and rinse hair several times.

Deep Conditioning

Dry, brittle hair: Hot oil: warm two tbsp olive oil and massage gently into the scalp. Wrap a hot towel around the head, or wrap your hair in cling-film. Leave to cool on the head, then shampoo and rinse.

HOW TO LIVE ON LESS

Shine and lustre: Shake together 100 ml (3½ fl oz) olive oil and 200 ml (7 fl oz) liquid honey and allow to steep for a couple of days. Massage into the scalp and comb through. Wrap head as above, shampoo and rinse.

Dandruff: Add one tsp antiseptic in the final rinse water or make an infusion of cleavers. Rub a mixture of one part apple juice to three parts water into the scalp 2–3 times a week

Eyes

Eyes need gentle treatment but repay you with sparkle and liveliness.

Puffy eyes: Try adding another pillow to avoid pooling of fluid around the eyes as you sleep.
Apply iced water or cold milk with a cotton wool ball.
Grated potato or pulped strawberries under the eyes reduces swelling.

Tired eyes: Two rings of cucumber are classic, but slices of washed and peeled potato are equally good – both are very effective if you can keep them still as your eyeballs move under them!
As an alternative that stays in place a little better, try using compresses of two used chamomile teabags which you have allowed to go cold: place over the eyes for about 15 minutes and relax – and you get a double-whammy of goodness if you drink the hot tea before you go to bed, as it will help you sleep.

Inflamed eyes: Fresh cucumber juice as eye drops; compresses of chamomile, eyebright or fennel seed.

Mouthwash

Home-made mouthwash is easy to prepare and tastes good too! It doesn't take your breath away as some commercial mouthwashes do, nor does it leave you with that tingly, anaesthetised feeling.

HOME AND LEISURE

Pour 600 ml (1 pint) boiling water over a combination of rosemary, anise and mint leaves, or a handful of blackcurrant or bramble leaves, and steep for 30 minutes. Cool, strain, bottle and label. It will keep in the fridge for several days. Use to rinse your mouth, swishing around your teeth and gums, after brushing.

Skin Freshener

- Add one tsp cider vinegar to 300 ml ($1/2$ pint) water; use as a liquid toner.
- Rub the skin gently with a slice of raw potato.
- Squeeze juice of two cucumbers, boil, skim, cool and bottle. Keeps for a few days in the fridge.

Moisturiser

Grind 25 g (1 oz) skinned almonds (you may need to blanch them several times to get their coats off) to a powder and slowly add 300 ml ($1/2$ pint) distilled water until you have a milky liquid; strain and use.

Face Masks

Try out the following tasty face masks using produce from your own garden. Clean your face and then apply one of the following for 20 minutes, then rinse with warm water.

- crushed strawberries on their own or with a handful of oatmeal
- mashed cucumber on its own
- mix 2 tbsp natural yoghurt with enough oatmeal to make a stiff paste, then stir in finely chopped herbs or flowers of your choice, e.g. lavender (stimulating), thyme (toning), marigold (astringent), yarrow (cleansing), marsh mallow (emollient)
- cucumber juice with $1/4$ tsp lemon juice, 1 tsp witch hazel, 1 tsp alcohol, one whipped egg white
- for oily skin: beat up an egg white until frothy – add $1/4$ tsp lemon juice or vinegar if you wish
- for oily skin: pulped pears
- for dry skin: beat up an egg yolk with 1 tbsp olive oil and few drops vinegar (mayonnaise!)
- for very dry skins: melt butter and beat in 2 tbsp milk: apply to face and leave for a few hours
- for any skin: beat together 1 tsp honey with 2 tbsp single cream; alternatively just use raw honey – sticky but effective!

Facial Steam

Stimulating and revitalising, take a facial steam once per week, unless you have a heart condition, asthma or visible red veins. It opens the pores to push out dirt and impurities.

Fill a large bowl or the sink with just-boiled water, then add an essential oil or a fresh or dried herb of your choice (see below). The hot water draws out the essential oils of herbs that not only help to heal your skin, they also influence mood. Cover your head and neck with a big towel and lean over the steam for about five minutes. Pat skin dry and apply moisturiser.

Dry skin:	evening primrose oil; dried elderflower and tansy flowers; dried tansy and lemon verbena leaves; fresh chamomile, lady's mantle, nettle, rosemary or thyme leaves
Normal to dry:	lavender or chamomile essential oil; dried chamomile, lavender, lemon balm, mint and thyme leaves
Normal to oily:	fresh mint leaves and a curl of lemon peel; alendula flowers; dried sage and yarrow leaves
For healing:	comfrey or fennel leaves

Herbal Baths

- To add fragrance to a bath, use eight drops of essential oil (see below) mixed with one tablespoon of semi-skimmed milk, which helps disperse the oil evenly through the water.
- To make an invigorating, fragrant bath, boil together equal parts white vinegar and water, then add two handfuls of fresh herbs (see below); leave to steep and cool before you add to the bath.
- Adding a handful of Epsom salts to either mixture will provide a therapeutic mineral bath – soaking your body in salts encourages your skin to release toxins and can help to relieve tired muscles.

Choose fresh herbs or essential oils that match your skin type.

Greasy skin:	lavender, orange, lemon, cypress, bergamot
Normal skin:	palma rosa, roman chamomile, jasmine, neroli, ylang-ylang, frankinsence, sandalwood, patchouli
Sensitive skin:	geranium, lavender, German chamomile
Dry or damaged skin:	geranium, lavender, clary sage, myrrh

HOME AND LEISURE

Nourishing Wash Bag
- Cut the foot off an old pair of tights, or use a knee-high sock.
- Fill the pouch with a handful of oatmeal and optionally some soothing herbs like chamomile or lavender.
- Tie a knot in the open end of the pouch.

Use in the bath or shower. When wet it will produce a lovely creamy liquid that will clean and nourish skin without drying it. One wash bag will last one day maximum – you can keep it in a bag in the fridge if you intend to use it morning and night, but don't attempt to store it for longer, as it can accumulate bacteria.

All-over Body Oil
After your bath or shower, and before you are completely dry, massage a small amount of oil into your skin to keep it supple and protected.

Younger skins:	apricot kernel oil, coconut oil, hemp seed oil, wheat germ oil, olive oil
Mature skins:	avocado oil, evening primrose oil, rosa moqueta oil
Any skin type:	almond oil, cocoa butter, emu oil, jojoba

Exfoliating Scrubs
You should not need to exfoliate more than once per week.

Oily and Combination Skin
Make a simple exfoliating scrub for your body or face by putting a handful of brown sugar in a bowl and mixing it with a vegetable oil (e.g. olive oil) and honey. Gently massage into the skin, rinse thoroughly and pat dry. The honey can be replaced with the juice of half a lemon.

Normal to Dry Skin
Make a gentle exfoliator by combining a handful of ground oatmeal with olive oil and honey and use as above. The honey can be replaced with a pulped peach.

Foot Bath
In a bowl large enough to take both your feet, throw in some herbs, e.g. rosemary, bay, lovage, marjoram, and add boiling water. Allow the herbs to steep for 15 minutes, throw in a handful of sea salt, then top up with cold water until you have a relaxing temperature. Just add tired feet!

Natural Pest Control (Indoors)

> ⓘ Did you know...? You can hire an environmentally friendly rodent control service by Mousers at www.cats.org.uk.

Having pests in the home can be upsetting as well as potentially harmful. In general, good hygiene and simple precautions should keep out unwanted visitors.

> Six of the Best: Practical ideas to reduce the likelihood of pests in the home.
>
> - Even if your food is in a cupboard or fridge, always keep it in tightly sealed jars or plastic boxes, not open packets. Many of today's packets have re-sealing capabilities – make sure they work properly.
> - Keep floors and surfaces, including chopping boards and inside drawers and cupboards clean – get rid of any crumbs and splashes quickly.
> - Vacuum floors regularly.
> - Rinse empty cans and cartons before they disappear for recycling – particularly if your collection is only every couple of weeks and you need to store them in the home.
> - Keep both internal and external rubbish bins covered; empty internal bins regularly.
> - Seal any cracks in walls, floors, skirting that might harbour insects or larger pests.

However, even with the best cleaning regime in the world, some little monsters will inevitably get in one day and there are a number of low-toxicity home-prepared methods you can use to get rid of them:

Ants:	Crush and sprinkle pennyroyal, sage, mint, thyme or bay leaves, paprika or cinnamon across ant paths, or rub pennyroyal until it releases it juices onto the surface (and particularly into any cracks) where you have an infestation.
Clothes moths:	Freeze woollies for 2–3 days; wash other clothing at high temperature.
Fleas:	Vacuuming ought to be enough, but if they come in with your pets, then deal with them on your pets. You can make an effective deterrent by soaking dog and cat collars (or in

HOME AND LEISURE

Flies:	fact just washing the whole animal!) in a strong infusion of rosemary leaves.
	Keep them out of the kitchen by keeping a basil plant on the windowsill. If they are particularly persistent, rub the basil leaves to release more of its aroma. Hang bags of dried lavender (or make lavender hangers) in wardrobes; push tea-bag-sized muslin bags with dried lavender in among clothes in drawers.
Mosquitoes:	Create a breeze with a fan; prepare a room spray using 115 ml (4 fl oz) water and essential oil (citronella, lemongrass, peppermint); use a mosquito net.
Rodents:	Cats catch mice; terriers catch rats; alternatively you will need traps to catch them and, finally, poison if you need to kill them.

We keep rodents out of our garage, storeroom and attic with an ultrasonic device, which is plugged into the mains and has a range of around 2,000 sq ft. It works by transmitting a pulse through the electrical wiring that irritates the nervous system of rodents, encouraging them to leave our house and look for somewhere more comfortable to live. See www.martleyelectronics.co.uk or www.pestcontrolshop.co.uk for a range of different pest-control products.

Arts and Crafts

There are so many arts and crafts that I couldn't begin to do the subject justice in this book. I myself am an off-and-on seamstress, and when I put my mind to it I can make my own skirts and dresses so long as I don't attempt anything too fancy. It does mean that every summer I have at least one or two new items to wear for my holiday that make me feel proud to have made myself and which are completely unique.

All crafts are fun and, when successful, incredibly satisfying. It's just a question of finding the right pastime that you will enjoy and that will produce a useful result. You never know, your pastime could even be the start of a small cottage industry – I know several people who have started small businesses in just this way. Hopefully you will recognise something in the list below that you'd like to attempt – you may have already tried a particular craft at school, or with your children, and so have a modicum of skill already, or you may like to reduce the amount you purchase of a particular item, e.g. candles, or even recycle material, e.g. to make new clothes or a patchwork quilt.

- basketry – willow baskets, rush work, raffia coil
- fabrics – dressmaking, patchwork, quilting, appliqué, rag dolls
- glass and metals – etching, stained glass, mosaic
- jewellery – beads, semi-precious stones, wire, shells
- leather – bags, belts, stuffed toys
- modelling – pottery, papier mâché, candles
- needlework – cross-stitch, crochet, embroidery
- paints and dyes – batik, potato printing, tie-dying, watercolours, oil painting, stencils
- wood – modelling, carving, sculpture, carpentry
- wool – knitting, weaving, rug making, macramé

✂ If you have latent talent, but need to improve upon it to be able to produce goods of a higher quality, why not take a class? Local councils provide a very broad range of practical classes, and a recognised qualification will go a long way to enabling you to sell your skills on a commercial basis. Otherwise, see if there is someone in your *Community Network* with whom you could trade a class for a skill or a service you could offer in return.

chapter 4

Food, Drink and a Few Bits More

This chapter is unashamedly focused on self-sufficiency, as it lends itself to a vast range of consumables that you can grow, raise or gather for yourself. That's not to say the other techniques in our toolkit aren't valid – hopefully the ideas in the "Saving Money" section at the beginning of the chapter will demonstrate how these too do their bit to help you live on less. It's just that growing your favourite vegetables or collecting berries from a hedgerow is so simple, cheap and rewarding that it should be a key part of your living-on-less strategy.

Not got a garden? No worries. I've included a small number of growing ideas that would work on the windowsill or even on a patio, balcony or garage roof.

Too much garden and/or no time or inclination to use it? Why not rent out part of your space or share with someone locally who would like to grow fruit and vegetables – you could come to some arrangement with the resultant produce.

> HOW TO LIVE ON LESS

Saving Money on Everyday Consumables

Reality Check: ♈ ① (£-)

Shopping

✘ OK, folks, we're off to the shops (or to the PC for *Online Shopping*). First thing's first – make a list. This is essential *Budgeting and Planning* for this chapter, as it will help keep you disciplined to buy only what you need, when you need it. But don't just write down "three lunches, three dinners, milk, bread and cereals", as this isn't focused enough. Have a *Plan* of what you are going to eat for the week, or at least the next few days, taking into account how you will use any leftovers, and then develop the shopping list to reflect these decisions. Knowing what you are planning to cook can also help steer you clear of ready-made food – you can produce something much cheaper and more nutritious if you cook from scratch. The list idea should also be used for the garden centre – and here's where I need to take my own advice, as buying plants is where I notoriously overspend!

✘ Getting the *Timing* right for your shopping can make a difference to the amount you spend. There are often end-of-day bargains in the supermarket, seasonal *Multi-Purchase Deals* at the garden centre, and pre-holiday bargains before stores are closed for extended periods when perishables need to be offloaded, e.g. Christmas Eve, Maundy Thursday, etc. Ian and I happened on this trend quite by chance when we first lived together and managed to fill up our freezer one Christmas Eve with numerous joints of heavily-discounted meat. Post-Christmas there is often a sale of Christmas specialities (if you can still bear the sight of them!) – cakes, mince pies, sausage rolls, puddings, turkeys, etc. – great if you are planning a party and/or can fill up the freezer. The garden centres, quite apart from selling plants, also tend to sell off their Christmas decorations at this time, so you could pick up some bargains ready for next year.

✘ It may just be worth knowing, as you browse through in the *Stores and Outlets*, a bit of the psychology behind supermarket shelving. The most profitable items (for the store), and indeed the easiest for the customer to access, are put at eye level and at the ends of the aisle, where you naturally slow down to turn the corner. Be aware of this and let your eyes move to the upper and lower shelves as well to source products that may be better value. Always ask for help if you can't reach an item you want from the

FOOD, DRINK AND A FEW BITS MORE

top shelf, or don't want to bend down to lift from the bottom shelf. Be cautious also of the Multi-Purchase Deals available in these areas – they are there to tempt you to buy more, not spend less, so only select the multi-buy if it's exactly what you need.

✂ *Budget supermarkets.* You know the ones I mean? They generally have box-like shapes with no windows. And inside they pile 'em high and sell 'em cheap. Get to know what they sell, and at what price, so that you can at least carry the knowledge with you when shopping at your preferred supermarket.

✂ *Multi-purchase Deals.* Buy-one-get-one-free (BOGOF) is a difficult deal to avoid, particularly if the produce is the same price as it usually is, but you are getting twice the quantity. Other Multi-purchase Deals like "2 for £5" or "3 for the price of 2" work well if the product that is discounted is something you always buy and need a large quantity of. Otherwise, stop and think whether you need two or just one. Buying two doesn't "save" you £2.70 (or whatever) if it's something you don't need or can't use before it deteriorates; quite the reverse. I find that sometimes I'm left with significantly more produce than the two of us can sensibly consume before it perishes, so then it gets wasted, which is something I really, really hate. The answer is you need to have a strategy for dealing with excess, for example:

- Freeze what you don't need immediately while raw.
- Cook the produce then freeze…the home-made version of a "ready meal".
- Share with a friend.
- Leave the second/third packet on the shelf (which, if it's a BOGOF offer, seems a waste of a deal, but someone else might be better equipped than you to benefit from it).

✂ *Own brand.* If your family is fussy, introduce one or two own brands at a time, explain why you are doing it (because hopefully you are living-on-less as a family-wide decision, so they should be supportive if not encouraging), and let them get used to the new products gradually – some they will hopefully accept, others they may well rebel against! Goods that are going into casseroles anyway – tinned tomatoes, beans, etc. – can easily be replaced with a cheaper, own brand variety, as the taste of the finished dish will have more to do with your cooking skills and the other flavourings you will add like seasoning, herbs and spices than the quality of the tomatoes. Basics and staples like flour, sugar, washing-up liquid and soap are often good candidates for "own brand" treatment, as they don't upset the family quite so much as the loss of their favourite ketchup.

✖ *Online shopping*, either direct or through a *Cashback Portal*, means you don't have the hassle of going to the shops, going back and forth round the aisles looking for that elusive jar of capers (or whatever), or carrying your goods to/from the car. Deliveries are generally offered until late at night in convenient 15-minute intervals. I've never been disappointed with this shopping technique – but I have to say I still prefer to go to the shops just to look and see.

✖ Supermarkets, both their physical outlets and their online equivalents, are a major user of *Loyalty Cards*, and you should make sure you have one for your preferred outlet(s). As the points build up, swap them for your choice of:

- money off your bill
- Air Miles
- discounted days out
- or whatever takes your fancy

Garden centres similarly operate their own schemes, though typically not linked in to the major programmes like the supermarkets. Nevertheless, they offer a good way to save money off your future purchases if you intend to shop regularly at the same centre. Both the garden centres I frequent that have loyalty schemes provide vouchers to trade against your next purchase, but one additionally sends a "birthday" voucher and a big paper bag to fill up with spring bulbs for free.

Cooking and Eating

Changing your habits isn't a theme that has particularly cropped up before, and it didn't get a mention in the toolkit at the beginning of the book. However, simply changing how you cook and what you eat can have a remarkable impact on your finances.

Even with a busy 7 am to 7 pm city job with frequent overseas travel, I have always found the time to cook meals from scratch. I think it's largely because I enjoy it, and I like to know exactly what's going inside me, but also because during a mad few months of my life I did actually go down the ready-made

FOOD, DRINK AND A FEW BITS MORE

meals route as a misguided means of gaining time in the evening. Apart from the fact that the grocery bill increased immediately and I don't think I actually gained any spare time, I started to get tired, my weight began to increase, I started to under-perform at work, and I couldn't be bothered to go to the gym. I looked critically at my diet in an attempt to reverse the bad effects and decided to ditch the ready-mades at the same time as increasing the amount of fresh fruit, vegetables and pulses we ate, in an effort to put improved vitamins, minerals and protein back into my body. Everything improved within days of getting back on track.

If you're an avid consumer of ready-made food or cook-in-sauces, but keen to pursue a living-on-less and/or healthy living strategy, why not start to reduce your dependence on pre-cooked food by attempting to prepare one or two of your favourite meals from scratch? Pasta, curries, mince-based dishes, roasted vegetables, omelettes, fish, or chops/steaks with two or three vegetables needn't take more than 20 to 30 minutes from start to finish. And while that's on the go, you can prepare a delicious fruit crumble for dessert (no need to cook the fruit first!) or a fresh fruit salad (which can double-up for breakfast, either as-is or whizzed into a smoothie). Slower-cooked dishes like bean bakes, casseroles and some roasted joints of meat take no more time to prepare but longer to cook. Whenever you bake for extended periods, always make sure the oven is full and try to use the residual heat once cooking is complete, e.g. to warm things up like cooked (left-over) dessert or fruit pies, to dry meringues or herbs, or possibly even to set the new papier maché model you've just created. With organisation (and maybe a slow cooker that cooks while you're at work), cooking from scratch need not be as daunting or as time-consuming as you may think – you might even enjoy it! It will certainly help you live on less.

If meat is your most costly food item, then why not replace one or two meals (or "extend" a dish if the family really won't give up their meat) with pulses – beans or lentils – or products made from soya. The dried versions of all pulses are the most economical – you can get a 1 kg bag of red lentils for £1.63 – but may require some organisation to soak overnight and cook before you add to the dish. All pulses are also available in tins. No advance preparation is needed, but they are not quite as cheap – though at 35p for 235 g (drained weight), they are still a fraction of the cost of meat. If you need to "disguise" lentils in a dish, use red lentils if you want them to completely disintegrate into a soup, curry or pasta sauce, or brown lentils if you want them to resemble mince in a shepherd's pie or

Bolognese sauce. Otherwise, draw inspiration from some of the numerous international meat-and-bean dishes like Mexican chilli con carne, French cassoulet, Dutch bean soup or Chinese stir-fry with bean sprouts (which you can sprout yourself – see later in the Self-sufficiency section).

Stocking the Garden

I find it incredibly easy to go over the budget I set myself at the beginning of the year when it comes to the garden – I am so greedy for plants and I like to try and grow new varieties of vegetable whenever I can.

✻ The garden is one area where it's easy to get the *Timing* right for your purchases, as garden centres are completely in tune with the seasons. This means *Budgeting and Planning* can be organised for the whole year, as you should be able to work out in advance what gaps need to be filled and what plants and seeds need to be purchased for the border and the fruit and vegetable patch. If you're starting a vegetable patch from scratch, take a look at the Self-sufficiency section below, which identifies how many plants of each type of vegetable you could grow to feed a family of four.

✻ *Plan* to take advantage of all the free seeds, cuttings, divisions, etc. that your garden will provide during the year – swap with friends and neighbours to diversify. You will find that most gardeners are keen to be thrifty and are willing to share their plants, and sometimes even their produce if you have something different to offer in return.

✻ As with other types of purchases, take advantage of *Online Shopping* – it's particularly useful if you are bulk buying a single item or you want to buy a specific cultivar or specimen plant – it certainly beats traipsing around all the garden centres only to find they don't have exactly what you want.

Last autumn we bought 75 beech hedge plants to fill the gaps in our immature hedge, together with a Rosa glauca to replace one (of a group of three) that had died – or, to be fair, that had been dug up by the !£$%^&* rabbits. Each had to be the exact match for its companions, so we needed to be very particular not just about selecting the right variety but also getting the right height and maturity to fit in with the others. We found several *Online Shopping* websites local to where we live that could fulfil our needs, all at reasonable costs and all with delivery within a few days. Very easy. And we are so pleased with the results we'll be returning to the site this spring to source some new plants.

FOOD, DRINK AND A FEW BITS MORE

Self-sufficiency

If you do just one thing: Do nothing! According to Cleve West, garden designer, you need just two square metres of uncut grass to generate enough oxygen for one human being for a year.

One of the cornerstones of self-sufficiency has to be the ability to provide your own food, whether it be fruit and vegetables from the garden or produce from livestock. We'll cover livestock later in this section, but right now I'll take you through setting up an area of the garden for you to grow seasonal, organic produce so that you can become self-sufficient, at least in your favourite fruit, vegetables and herbs, virtually the whole year round.

I've also included a section on cut flowers, so that your borders can do their bit for the self-sufficiency drive and double-up as beautiful outdoor displays, as well as provide year-round interest in vases. Compost is another key contributor to a self-sufficient lifestyle – both in terms of recycling kitchen and garden waste, as well as contributing to the structure and nutritive value of your soil. That's followed by three further sections: one covering natural pest control, so that you can see how easy it is to grow your food organically, another on home-made beverages, then finally the ultimate living-on-less strategy – food for free.

Even if you don't have a garden, there are a number of small projects you can undertake in the home, or on a balcony, patio or roof, that will allow you to grow a small amount of produce and make that all-important contribution towards self-sufficiency.

> Six of the Best: Self-sufficiency projects.
>
> - the productive garden: vegetables, fruit, herbs and flowers
> - natural pest control (outdoors)
> - compost
> - beverages
> - livestock
> - foraging

HOW TO LIVE ON LESS

The Productive Garden

Vegetables
No garden? No matter. Why not grow:

- salad leaves, herbs and vegetables in a window box
- sprouted beans and seeds on the windowsill
- tomatoes in a hanging basket
- potatoes in a tub/dustbin/tyre pile/wooden barrel
- courgettes in a tub – just one plant provides plenty for two people
- a vegetable garden in a grow-bag or two

The Indoor Salad Garden

Reality Check: ϒ ☺ £-

As a child I'm sure you will have tried growing mustard and cress on a piece of blotting paper. I know I did, but as I can't remember the results I can only assume the project wasn't successful, or perhaps didn't hold my attention for long enough.

These days, sprouting seeds or growing them on to micro-greens or baby leaf salads has become a rewarding pastime, as well as providing a year-round supply of delicious pest-free salad ingredients for just a few pence – highly nutritious and a good contribution to living on less.

Sprouting Beans and Seeds
Packed with protein, vitamins, minerals and amino acids, seeds and beans are already an important and cheap addition to our diet. Once germinated, their nutritional value increases and provides interesting colour, flavour and texture to our food.

And they're really easy to sprout – just add water!

Equipment
A container to grow your sprouts in, e.g.:

- large clear glass jar plus a pair of tights or muslin to cover and use as a strainer
- tray – the best container for sprouts that need greening
- hessian or linen bag (for sprouts that don't need greening)

FOOD, DRINK AND A FEW BITS MORE

Plus some water and a little bit of TLC.

Method

Put the seeds or beans in their container, remembering that they are going to triple in size, and soak for 8–12 hours or overnight. Once the beans or seeds have absorbed as much water as they can by soaking, drain thoroughly and set them in a dark but warm place to germinate – 21–24°C (70–75°F) is optimal – and begin the process of twice-daily rinsing and draining. Make absolutely sure all moisture is drained from the seeds. Use some kitchen towel if necessary to soak up the remaining drops of water – otherwise your seeds will quickly go mouldy. If you are using a linen or hessian sack, simply dip this into a bucket of water, then hang and leave to drain. After a couple of days you can move your sprouts into the light, but avoid direct sunlight unless it's really cold. Seeds are ready when their coats start to fall off.

What to Sprout

There is a wide range of seeds, pulses and grains that you can try. Some common ones are:

Seed/Bean	Container	Notes	Harvest
Aduki	Bag	Crispy and sweet. Use for stir-fries, salads, soups, sandwiches and for juicing.	5 days
Alfalfa	Tray or Jar	Mild taste. A so-called "super food". Use for salads, juices, sandwiches and finger food.	7 days
Chickpea	Bag	Needs cooking. Use for hummus, in salads, stir-fries and casseroles.	4 days
Clover	Tray or Jar	Like alfalfa but a sharper taste.	6 days
Fenugreek	Tray or Jar	Bitter – use sparingly.	9 days
Lentil	Bag	Steam or add to salads.	5 days
Mung	Bag	The classic Chinese bean sprout. Salads, stir-fries and juicing.	5 days
Mustard	Tray or Jar	Hot – use sparingly.	6 days
Pea	Bag	Needs cooking.	5 days

Alternatively, why not collect seeds from your own crops – coriander, radish, sunflowers – and sprout those as well.

Micro-greens

Micro-greens are salad leaves or vegetables harvested when their first leaves have appeared, generally within 7–10 days. They have a more intense flavour than the mature versions of the plant and so don't need to be used in huge quantities. They're very fashionable at the moment – used in posh restaurants as salads and as a garnish – and consequently very expensive to buy! Growing your own costs next to nothing and is very easy.

Method
- Soak some felt or hessian.
- Sow your chosen salad leaf (or vegetable) as evenly as you can over the soaked cloth.
- Stand on a sunny windowsill or better still in a greenhouse at a constant temperature of 18–22°C (65–72°F).
- Cover for a couple of days to accelerate germination.
- Uncover to start the greening-up process.
- Provide moisture every day in the form of mist or water to the base, but don't waterlog.
- After 7–10 days, according to the variety, harvest by cutting close to the base.
- If required, keep cut leaves in a plastic bag in the fridge for 2–3 days.

This is a good method for amaranth, basil, beetroot, broccoli, coriander and rocket.

Baby Leaf and Mature Leaf Salad
Instead of harvesting micro-greens when the first leaves have appeared, continue growing for a further couple of weeks to develop baby leaf salad; mature leaves will be ready from about eight weeks.

Outdoors: Growing Vegetables and Salad Crops

Reality Check: ⚹ ⚹ ☺☺ £- £+ ♥

> ⓘ Did you know...? If you scratch a bar of soap until your fingernails are completely full of soap, the garden dirt doesn't get under your nails.

Grow your favourite vegetables in a dedicated plot, your flower border, in a tub or in a grow-bag just to get yourself started with growing vegetables and tasting the difference that home-grown organic vegetables provide. You don't need to plant in a row if you don't have the space – just block-plant at the appropriate distance (see table), keep weeded and watered, and enjoy!

FOOD, DRINK AND A FEW BITS MORE

With careful planning, a little bit of skill and no amount of luck with the changing British climate, you can produce a regular stream of fresh, organic vegetables for the family from the vegetable garden – and all for a great deal less than you get buy them from the supermarket.

In my own garden I have set aside three small raised beds to grow enough vegetables for the two of us, but the basic idea is scalable if you have more space and/or mouths to feed. I grow what I know we both like, and I try to grow in the quantity I know we can consume without producing too much of a glut – though when there is more produce than we can sensibly consume without getting tired of eating the same vegetables, there's a range of easy recipes to preserve your vegetables for eating out of season. If you want deliberately to produce more than you can eat so that you have extra for sale, barter or preserving, then obviously you can increase the quantities I suggest.

I also stick wherever possible to organic methods, and these I will describe in the section on natural pest control, as I am conscious that what goes into the soil and onto the plants is eventually going to end up inside me and my loved ones. Some methods are more effective than others in my garden – they may be different in yours – and I've tried no end of methods to keep the predators off, some successful, others not. It's all part and parcel of the joy of organic vegetable gardening.

Designing the Vegetable Patch

If you do just one thing: Grow your favourite vegetable or salad.

The size of your vegetable patch will depend entirely on:

- how much available space you have in the garden
- the amount of space you want to dedicate to growing vegetables
- how many people you are trying to feed
- your desire to produce extra for preserving or gifting/selling/bartering

So you could have anything from an area the size of a grow-bag to something more akin to an allotment. Either way, the principles are the same.

The site for your vegetable garden should be light and airy. It should get plenty of sun and not be shaded by trees or high fences. Vegetables could be grown on a plot that gets shade for up to half of the day, but they won't crop as well.

Firstly, decide what you want to grow and eat. I will be suggesting quantities for the most popular vegetables to feed a family of four a little later in this section, but ultimately it's your choice.

Typically you will be choosing to grow vegetables of different types:

- brassicas
- courgettes and pumpkins
- herbs
- onions, shallots, garlic
- peas and beans
- roots
- salads – leaves, tomatoes, peppers

Some types of vegetables naturally grow well together – e.g. peas and beans – because they like to grow in the same conditions. In the case of peas and beans, they both fix nitrogen from the air and concentrate it in their roots. Others need to be given specific nutrients – e.g. brassicas are greedy for nitrogen, so they are a good follow-on crop once the peas and beans have been cleared and their roots dug into the soil. And then other crops like courgettes and salads really don't mind whom they share a bed with, and can largely be fitted in around other crops, filling gaps.

However, when you grow the same crop in the same location every year, it leaches the soil of the goodness it takes out and fixes the soil with the goodness it leaves behind. Therefore, the best way to grow vegetables is in an annual rotation, where one group of plants follows on from another, thus benefiting from the nutrients left behind and in turn adding value back into the soil. Rotation also disrupts the lifecycle of diseases and pests, thus helping you to grow stronger, healthier crops. Rotation is generally on a four-year basis, which is why vegetable growers have three or four beds (but you could have one single bed, divided into three/four areas).

Four-Year (Three- or Four-Plot) Crop Rotation Plan
Below I've suggested a four-year rotation plan: everything moves on each year and returns to its starting point in Year 4. You'll see it doesn't include crops like asparagus, rhubarb, tomatoes, salads, courgettes, peppers or chillies. This is because they don't need to be rotated and can either be fitted in anywhere you have space, or even dedicated to a fourth bed. Note that asparagus needs to stay in the same place for its lifetime – up to 20 years!

FOOD, DRINK AND A FEW BITS MORE

	Plot A	Plot B	Plot C
Year 1	Peas, Beans, Salad, Celery, Leeks, Radish, Spinach, Sweet corn	Potatoes, Beetroots, Carrots, Onions, Parsnips, Swedes, Turnips	Cabbages, Broccoli, Brussels sprouts, Cauliflower, Kale
Year 2	Cabbages, Broccoli, Brussels sprouts, Cauliflower, Kale	Peas, Beans, Salad, Celery, Leeks, Radish, Spinach, Sweet corn	Potatoes, Beetroots, Carrots, Onions, Parsnips, Swedes, Turnips
Year 3	Potatoes, Beetroots, Carrots, Onions, Parsnips, Swedes, Turnips	Cabbages, Broccoli, Brussels sprouts, Cauliflower, Kale	Peas, Beans, Salad, Celery, Leeks, Radish, Spinach, Sweet corn
Year 4	As Year 1	As Year 1	As Year 1

Planting Plan to Feed a Family of Four
In the following table I've indicated a vegetable planting plan to adequately feed a family of two adults and two children, providing plenty of variety and seasonality. Unless you have an allotment (lucky you!), or a particularly large plot, you're unlikely to be able to fit everything in that's on the list, so do sit down with a pencil and paper and draw up a scaled plan of precisely where each crop will go, taking into account how much space it takes up. If necessary, scale up or down to meet your circumstances. Later in this chapter I'm also going to suggest some companion plants, but these can generally be fitted in between rows of vegetables (great for suppressing the weeds…).

If you can, reserve a small part of your vegetable patch for experimenting with lesser-known varieties or a vegetable that is new to you. Whatever you decide to do, don't waste any space! Remember, crops like lettuce and herbs can be fitted in anywhere and are a better option than having bare soil.

Try to pick your crops fresh for each meal and eat them as soon as possible after they have been harvested. If you are freezing any surplus, get the vegetables cleaned up and in the freezer as quickly as you can to maintain as much nutritional value as possible.

HOW TO LIVE ON LESS

Vegetable	Quantity	Planting & Harvesting	Other Notes
Asparagus	Ten crowns, 45cm (18") apart.	Harvest every other day from the second season from mid-spring for about 6–8 weeks.	Takes two years to establish but stays in the same place for up to 20 years. Keep well weeded, but do it by hand, as the asparagus has a shallow root system. Packs of crowns come in tens, so why not share a batch with a friend or neighbour and grow two varieties.
Beans *Broad*	Two 3 m (10 ft) rows (plus one for the freezer, if needed), 45 cm (18") apart.	Direct sow seeds 20 cm (8") apart in the autumn or spring.	I always interplant mine with sweet peas as a companion plant. Keep an eye out for black fly infestation and pick out the tops if necessary.
French	Two 3 m (10 ft) rows.	Direct sow seeds 20 cm (8") apart, starting in April and ending in August, or add more rows if you want a surplus for freezing.	Keep well watered. Last year I under-planted mine with nasturtiums as a companion plant – I had a superb crop of nasturtiums (the peppery leaves go very well in a salad!) but unfortunately the bean harvest was poor. I am not deterred…
Runner	One double row, 30 cm (12") apart.	Pick beans every couple of days from July through to September.	Make sure you have a good supporting frame before you start and sow two seeds next to each upright.

FOOD, DRINK AND A FEW BITS MORE

Vegetable	Quantity	Planting & Harvesting	Other Notes
Beetroot	Two rows, 12" apart.	Direct sow seeds at intervals, starting in February for summer eating: you should get around 30–40 small beet; then plant another two rows, 30 cm (1 ft) apart, for autumn and winter use.	Dead easy, and delicious. You will need to thin apart when they are large enough. Reusing Seedlings: Replant seedlings – they will be slower growing than the original crop but should do well – or add to salads; as a minimum throw on the compost.
Broccoli, *Purple Sprouting*	Ten plants per planting; three plantings.	Pick heads without any large leaves.	Take up a fair amount of space for a relatively small quantity of crop.
Brussels Sprouts	Six rows, 45 cm (18") apart.	Plant even closer so that they provide a mutual support system.	Aim for 20 early, 20 mid-season and 20 late maturing plants, otherwise you'll have a lot of sprouts all at the same time!
Cabbages *Spring*	Twelve plants 30 cm. (18") apart	Some to eat as spring greens, allowing others to heart up.	I plant dill with my cabbages as a companion plant.
Summer, autumn	2–3 rows planted 45 cm (18 in) apart.	Should produce 20–25 heads.	One cabbage will easily feed a family of four with some left over for soups or bubble and squeak. Trim the cabbage of coarse outer leaves first.
Winter	Twelve plants 45 cm (18") apart.	Each should achieve a finished weight of 1.25 – 1.75 kg (3–4 lb).	

HOW TO LIVE ON LESS

Vegetable	Quantity	Planting & Harvesting	Other Notes
Carrots *Early*	Two rows.	Direct sow seeds in succession from February through to August.	I always interplant rows of spring onion and radish with my carrots. Thin out to 2.5 cm (1") apart – see Beetroot for notes on reusing seedlings.
Main crop	Two rows, 20 cm (8") apart.		You may need to provide a barrier around your carrots to deter carrot fly.
Cauliflowers	Plant 12 heads in spring and summer.		Cauliflowers grow really large and I find I only need one every other week or so. A 1 kg (2 1/4 lb) head with leaves trimmed will serve four people, with some to spare for adding to soups and curries or for eating raw with dips.
Celery	One row, 1 m (3 ft) wide.	25 plants in succession 15 – 22 cm (6–9 in) apart.	For braising you will need two heads for four people. Great to serve with a cheese board, eat raw in salads or as crudités with dips.
Chard	Two 3 m (10 ft) rows, one in spring, one in late summer.	Thin seedlings to 15 cm (6") to 15 cm (6") apart – see Beetroot for notes on reusing seedlings.	An unusual vegetable but highly productive: use like spinach, i.e. raw in salads, lightly stir-fried or steamed. Cut enough leaves with scissors as you need them.
Courgettes	Plant four courgette plants 1 m (3 ft) apart.	Leave a couple of weeks between each planting and choose different varieties. I challenge you not to get a glut of courgettes! Be prepared to pick one every day.	Grow like topsy and are really delicious. They take up a lot of space (1 metre diameter), but they're worth it. Last year I came back from a two-week holiday and found the most monstrously large vegetables I've ever seen…but they still tasted great in a courgette pie or a curry, and I'm sure any domestic goddess could make sublime chutney!

FOOD, DRINK AND A FEW BITS MORE

Vegetable	Quantity	Planting & Harvesting	Other Notes
Garlic	Three heads, divided into cloves.	Plant cloves point uppermost 7.5 cm (3") deep and 15 cm (6") apart.	Needs a spell of cold weather. I generally plant mine chequerboard-style rather than in a long line. To store, plait the leaves together à la French bicycle rider and hang in a cool, dry place.
Kale	Plant three rows of different kale varieties in June about 30 cm (1 ft) apart.	Pick while young, cutting off leaves with scissors.	My husband and I adore cavolo nero, the black version of kale, but despite regular appearances several years ago in the stores it has suddenly been quite difficult to find. Now we grow it ourselves.
Leeks	Direct sow three rows of seeds 8 cm (3") apart, or drop seedlings sow into very deep holes then back fill with water.	The closeness of the spacing allows the leeks to self-blanch. Alternatively, further apart and "heap up" the soil around the plant as it grows.	Allow one well-grown leek per person if provided as a sautéed vegetable. Leave leeks in the ground through the winter until you need them.
Lettuce (and other salad leaves)	Direct sow a row of lettuce once a month from March.	Thin to allow each plant to grow to about 20–25 cm (8–10") across – see Beetroot for notes on reusing seedlings. Don't "lift" the salad leaves – just cut as much as you want down to the base and the plant will regenerate.	Dead easy to grow and a great "filler" crop wherever there is space. Alternatively, grow in rows or chequerboard – if you use a combination of salad types you can achieve an attractive colour palate just with lettuce. I like to grow mine behind the beans and sweet corn, which provide a decent amount of shade to the tender leaves. Oriental leaves typically over-winter well and cannot tolerate summer conditions.

HOW TO LIVE ON LESS

Vegetable	Quantity	Planting & Harvesting	Other Notes
Mangetout	Direct sow a row of seed in November and then another in March, about 15 cm (6") apart.	Thin out if you need to – see Beetroot for notes on reusing seedlings.	Supply some kind of twiggy support (I use willow branches, because I have a lot of them) for them to climb over. Mangetout like a long drink when the drought kicks in.
Onions, Spring Onions, Shallots			
Spring	Several rows.	Sow in succession between other crops.	Spring onions make a very neat row of quick-growing vegetables – I often use them as a natural, edible divider between other crops like carrots, beetroot and onions.
Main crop	Purchase onion sets (typically by the 50) in late autumn.	Plant in long rows or chequerboard style, as many as you think you might need.	I like to plant white and red onions as well as shallots. Onions store very easily, so although you will end up with several tens of kg worth of onions, they will see you through the winter and spring.
Parsnips	Two rows, 20 cm (8") apart 7.5 cm (3") between plants	Direct sow 2 cm (3/4") deep.	Don't plant on a windy day – the seeds are so light and airy they just fly out of the packet. Thin seedlings when they get large enough to handle – see Beetroot for notes on reusing seedlings.
Peas	Six rows (three early, three main crop), 60 cm (2 ft) between rows.	5 cm (2 in) between seeds. This should give a decent surplus for freezing.	Plant different varieties: young and main crop peas. Use some twiggy support (I use willow twigs because I have a number of willows that get cut down each February).

FOOD, DRINK AND A FEW BITS MORE

Vegetable	Quantity	Planting & Harvesting	Other Notes
Potatoes	3 kg (6.6 lb) of seed potatoes for every three rows.	Produces 22.7–31.7 kg (50–70 lb) of earlies and up to 45 kg (100 lb) of second early and main crop varieties.	A lot depends upon the variety and the season.
Radishes	Several rows of, about 15 cm (6 in) between rows.	Direct sow seeds in succession; can be planted between other crops like carrot or beetroot.	One of the quickest growing crops, I use them as a catch crop and as a natural, edible divider between crops. Last year I failed to lift some and ended up with some tennis-ball sized radishes – they were delicious grated into a salad!
Spring Greens	Plant 20–30 plants in the summer, according to how many you think you might want.	Pick as needed throughout the winter.	Quick to grow, hardy through the winter and very tasty!
Spinach	One row every couple of months from spring.	Direct sow seeds in succession.	Easy to grow as a cut-and-come-again crop. Like lettuce, cut with scissors down to the base and the plant will regenerate several times. Cover your final sowing (September) with a cloche to maintain a crop throughout the winter.
Swedes	Two rows, 45 cm (18 in) between rows.	Direct sow seeds 15 cm (6 in) apart.	Yuck, horrid, can't stand them! But you might like them…
Squash	Plant two different species.	Many of them produce lots of small fruits rather than a small number of large ones.	Squash needs to be given a lot of moisture, so prepare the soil well and keep watered. Excellent ground cover plant under taller crops like beans and sweet corn.

HOW TO LIVE ON LESS

Vegetable	Quantity	Planting & Harvesting	Other Notes
Sweet corn	Twenty plants.	Arranged chequerboard style so that they create a solid barrier providing shade and protection for other plants.	Keep well watered. I plant my sweet corn along with broad beans and squash – the "Three Sisters" so-called by the North American Indians.
Tomatoes	10–12 plants, 60 cm (2 ft) apart.	If you can, buy 10–12 different cultivars so that you get a range of harvest times as well as different sizes and uses.	Under-plant with basil as a companion plan.
Turnips	Summer, two rows, 25 cm (10 in) apart. Winter, two rows, 30 cm (1 ft) apart.	Seedlings thinned to 10 cm (4 in) apart – see Beetroot for notes on thinning.	

FOOD, DRINK AND A FEW BITS MORE

Using Produce from your Vegetable Garden

Aga-Roasted Vegetable Crisps
Apologies for those of you who don't have an Aga, but I'm sure you can re-create the recipe in a regular hot oven...I've just never tried it. This is a favourite with my husband and me. The recipe allegedly serves 3 or 4...

Ingredients
2 carrots (make them nice fat ones)
2 large beetroot
2 parsnips
1 sweet potato
1 ordinary potato
About 2" butternut squash taken from the long end
Oil
Coarse salt and freshly ground black pepper

Method

1. Peel or scrape all the vegetables. Slice the vegetables thinly using the fine cutter on a mandoline (mind your fingers!).

   Shape doesn't matter, but size does! Cut quite large pieces so that you will be able to pick up individual crisps rather than pour crisp dust into your hand. I find that using my food processor for this task results in crisps that are too small – the mandoline slicer is more controllable.

   I tend to keep the vegetables separate as they have different moisture contents and cooking times differ slightly. Do the beetroot last of all as it makes a mess and might stain the other vegetables.

2. Grind coarse salt over both sides of the vegetables – this will help to draw out the moisture.

3. Blot out excess moisture from the vegetables with a paper towel then put in one layer in the simmering oven to dry out for 5–10 minutes.

4. Brush a roasting tray or baking sheet with oil.

5. Arrange the vegetables in a single layer and roast on the bottom of the roasting oven for about 5 minutes each side. Check after 3 or 4 minutes

to make sure none are burning – since each vegetable varies in moisture content depending on its thickness, it's not as exact a science as I'd like it to be

You will need to do several batches, so make sure the roasting tray is wiped clean (to mop up excess moisture) and re-oiled.

Roast the beetroot separately to avoid it colouring other vegetables.

6. Spread out on a cooling rack (I open out the Aga toaster over the hob) and then leave to go cold and crisp.

7. Sprinkle with salt, and pepper if liked.

Variations
Use oil flavoured with garlic, herbs or chilli to cook the vegetables. Sprinkle with spices (cumin is particularly good) or flavoured salt, e.g. garlic salt, celery salt.

Vegetable Stock (and Mid-morning Pick-me-up)

Ingredients
500-700 g (1-1½ lb) mixed fresh seasonal vegetables (carrots, celery, turnips, fennel, potato)
3 litres (5¼ pints) water
Parsley
4 bay leaves
3–4 cloves
1 tsp juniper berries

Method

1. Scrub the root vegetables and peel if necessary.

2. Cut the vegetables into very small pieces and put into a large saucepan.

3. Cover with cold water, add the herbs, bring to the boil, and then simmer for 30 minutes.

4. Leave the vegetables in the stock to cool, then store covered in a cool place. This can be kept for up to a week but typically it gets used within several days.

FOOD, DRINK AND A FEW BITS MORE

5. Strain off as much as you want for soups, sauces and casseroles, or just drink as a mid-morning pick-me-up.

6. The remaining vegetables can be used to prepare a second stock for cooking, but not for drinking.

Ian's Borscht (Beetroot Soup)
This is my husband's recipe for Borscht, which was the first meal he ever made for me. The only improvement I have made to it is to use home-grown organic vegetables. My Finnish girlfriend Margit told him at a dinner party that she thought it was so good it must have come out of a tin!

Ingredients
1 large onion, peeled and sliced
1 large carrot, peeled and grated
2 large beetroot, peeled and sliced
½ small red cabbage, shredded
1.25 litres (2 pints) stock
1 tbsp tomato puree
1 tbsp malt vinegar
1 tbsp sugar
Salt and freshly ground pepper
Soured cream to serve (optional)
Chopped dill to serve (optional)

Method

1. Put a small amount of the water into a saucepan, bring to the boil and "water-fry" the onion for about 5 minutes.

2. Add the carrot, beetroot and cabbage and cook for a further 5 minutes.

3. Add all the remaining ingredients except the soured cream and dill, bring to the boil, lower the heat and simmer for about an hour until the vegetables are cooked.

4. Adjust the seasoning if you need to.

5. Ladle into warm bowls, top with soured cream and dill if using, and serve.

HOW TO LIVE ON LESS

Courgette Pie

Ingredients
500 g (1 lb 2 oz) courgettes (or other marrow)
500 g (1 lb 2 oz) fresh tomatoes
50g (1¾ oz) onions, finely chopped
2 cloves garlic, finely chopped
Oil
Parsley, finely chopped
Basil, finely chopped
500 g (1 lb 2 oz) potatoes
2 tbsp milk
2 spring onions
50 g (1¾ oz) butter

Method

1. Slice the courgettes into 2 cm (1") rings or chunks, brush lightly with oil, and grill for 10 minutes each side until golden.

2. Meanwhile, peel and chop the potatoes and cook for about 20 minutes until ready for mashing.

3. Make a cross through each end of each tomato, pour over boiling water and leave to stand for 10 minutes before slipping the skins off; then chop tomatoes.

4. Put about 2 cm (1") water into a saucepan and "water-fry" the onions for 5 minutes, then add the garlic and continue cooking for a further 3 minutes.

5. Add the chopped tomatoes, cover and cook for about 10 minutes until the tomatoes are reduced.

6. Add the courgettes, parsley and basil.

7. Mash the potatoes with a little milk and butter, then stir in the spring onions.

8. Place the courgette and tomato mix on the bottom of a buttered dish and top with the mashed potato.

9. Bake at 200°C (400°F, Gas Mark 6) for about 25 minutes or until golden.

Variations

- Add cream cheese with garlic and herbs to the mashed potato.
- Top the mashed potato with grated hard cheese.
- Use aubergines in place of courgettes.

Candied Pumpkin

450 g (1 lb) sugar
400 ml (14 fl oz) water
3 cinnamon sticks, broken up
Juice of 1 orange
1 kg (2¼ lb) pumpkin cut into 5 cm (2") chunks – no need to peel
Ground cinnamon for sprinkling

1. Put the sugar and water into a large, shallow pan with the cinnamon sticks and orange juice and heat gently until the sugar has dissolved completely.

2. Bring to the boil and carefully add the pumpkin. Reduce the heat and simmer gently for about 1–2 hours until the pumpkin is tender and the liquid has reduced to a thick glaze and coats the pumpkin.

3. Place the pumpkin on a serving plate and chill until ready to serve. Sprinkle with ground cinnamon just before serving.

Fruit

Reality Check: ϒ ☉ ££- ❤

I have to confess I'm a bit of a novice when it comes to fruit gardening. When I first met my husband, two gorgeous mature apple trees dominated his postage-stamp garden. Unfortunately, he had also developed an intolerance towards raw apples, so we just had to use the harvest to make gallons and gallons of home-made wine. We still have some in the attic. In my new garden – I call it "new" but actually we've been cultivating our site for five years – I have recently planted some raspberry canes, a couple of blackcurrant bushes and a goosegog, because they're the fruit I adore.

HOW TO LIVE ON LESS

Last year we only got a harvest from one of the blackcurrant bushes – we had two currants, to be precise, so at least we had one each! I also have a crab apple tree which has yet to produce fruit, and two mature walnut trees which supply me with more than enough walnuts to keep me in Waldorf salad, crumble topping and pesto for the whole year and the local squirrels with all they can carry away.

I would love an orchard, but that will have to wait for another time, perhaps even another place. In the meantime I marvel at what my friends and family produce from their own fruit trees and shrubs with what appears to be a relatively small amount of effort and not much space. Certainly when you weigh up the time and effort between vegetable gardening and fruit gardening, the latter is more relaxed until harvest time comes, when the fruit and nuts simply fall off the trees by the bucket-load and you need to be ready to eat, store or preserve. Also, you really don't need very much space, as my husband's former garden testifies – it's just a question of choosing the right size and form to fit your garden.

No Garden?

No matter. There are a number of patio or indoor fruit-growing projects that you could try, for example:

- Strawberries do well and look attractive in a hanging basket, or in a dedicated terracotta strawberry planter (pot with lots of holes up the sides). Also look out for "Double-Decker Table Top" supports from Ken Muir that can hold two tiers of grow-bags and ten strawberry plants – that could produce around 10 kg (22 lb) strawberries per year. See www.kenmuir.co.uk.
- Plant a small fruit tree in a tub on the patio, balcony or any flat roof.
- Cordons or fans of several fruit varieties can be trained flat up against a sunny wall of the house or garage – leave enough space in front of them to be able to harvest the crop and to access any windows.
- Keep citrus trees in the conservatory or a warm, sunny room.

Getting Started with a Fruit Garden

I am assuming that your fruit garden will be a key element of your living-on-less strategy, but what exactly do you hope to achieve?

- fresh fruit for eating in season, either raw or cooked
- surplus for freezing or storing straight after harvest for eating out of season

FOOD, DRINK AND A FEW BITS MORE

- regular supply of fruit juices and smoothies
- making jams and other preserves
- making wine
- mixture of some or all of the above

What you choose to grow will depend on what you want to achieve from the above list, plus:

- The amount of space you have to dedicate to a fruit garden. Is there just room for one specimen tree, or a few soft fruit bushes, or do you have a whole area that could be caged off against winged creatures and furry friends? Fruit can be planted in your flower border or vegetable patch – several varieties make useful dividers and screens – or you can train fruit bushes to cover unsightly structures like a fence, shed or garage.
- What fruits you and your family like to eat – tree fruit (apples, pears), stone fruit (plums, apricots), soft fruit (currants, berries), nuts (walnuts, hazelnuts).
- The local environment (sunny, exposed, soil depth and quality, etc.) in your garden and particularly the area(s) you have in mind for growing fruit.
- Whether the cultivars you choose need partner trees for pollination – either in your own garden or close by – or whether they are self-pollinating. They don't need to be the same variety for pollination, just be in flower at the same time.

Size Matters – So Does Shape

The eventual size of a fruit tree is determined by its rootstock. The same variety of fruit can be grown on a dwarf rootstock producing a plant of around 1.5 m (5 ft) – very easy for an adult to harvest and perfectly at home in a tub on the patio – or on a more vigorous rootstock to provide a dominating, tall tree that will be a focal point in the garden but will need a ladder to access the fruit.

The numerous methods of training fruit trees and bushes means you can choose what size and shape you plant and where. Raspberries on canes take up no more space than runner beans do in the vegetable garden (in fact, that's exactly where my raspberries are!). Gooseberries and redcurrants can either be grown as free-form bushes if you have the space, as fans or espaliers if you have a wall or a fence, or on a stem. An apple tree could be that beautiful, ornamental tree at the bottom of the garden, or some stepovers in the flower border. Note, however, that stepovers do get quite tall when mature, and will literally be a bit tricky to step over!

Check out the garden centres and fruit-growing books to see what height, width, shape and growing conditions your chosen fruit are available in, so that you select the varieties, forms and rootstock that suit your needs.

Quantity to Grow

The space you have will obviously dictate the number of fruit trees, bushes, fans, etc. you can grow. However, as a guide, here is an idea of how much to grow of some of the favourite fruit to keep a family of four happy through the year:

Apples	Three stepovers or cordons – they need not be the same variety if you want to spread harvest time – or one specimen tree.
Blackcurrants	At least two bushes – a blackcurrant should be productive for up to 10 years and produce between 4.5–6.75 kg (10–15 lb) of fruit each season.
Pears	Three stepovers or cordons – like apples you could plant different varieties – if you plant a tree you might have to wait a long time for it to become mature ("a pear for your heir").
Raspberries	Ten canes – select two different varieties so that they crop at different times – maybe one summer-fruiting, the other autumn-fruiting.
Strawberries	Very good ground cover! A dozen plants either in the ground or in a strawberry planter.

Where to Grow Fruit

Choose a site that will provide the maximum amount of sunshine as well as shelter from winds and frost, with good deep, fertile soil. Remember too that you will need a comfortable amount of space to be able to work around your plants for weeding, watering, pruning and harvesting.

Don't plant fruit trees where fruit trees used to be, as they may suffer from replant disease. The same, incidentally, is true of roses.

FOOD, DRINK AND A FEW BITS MORE

Using Produce from the Fruit Garden

Pear Sorbet

175g (6oz) caster sugar
300ml (10 fl oz) water
750 g (1lb 10oz) ripe dessert pears
1 tbsp lemon juice
2 egg whites (optional)
Poire William liqueur (optional)

Method

1. Peel the pears and stew in enough water to cover.

2. Remove the fruit pulp from the water and keep to one side; boil the remaining fluid rapidly until it reduces to 300 ml (10 fl oz).

3. Add the caster sugar and stir until dissolved; allow to cool.

4. Pass the pear pulp through a sieve and put into the sugar water; add the lemon juice.

5. Pour the mixture into polythene containers and freeze until semi-solid.

6. Remove from the freezer and whisk the mixture with a wire whisk to break up the ice.

6a. If using egg whites, whisk until the soft peak stage, then fold in the frozen pear pulp.

7. Return to the freezer until solid.

8. Ten minutes before serving, remove the sorbet from the freezer and mash with a fork to break it up.

9. Serve in individual glasses on its own or with 2 tsp Poire William liqueur poured over the sorbet.

Ian's Spicy Apple Chutney (Nau Ratan)

This is my husband's recipe for spicy apple chutney that we serve with a curry instead of commercially produced mango chutney. He tells me Nau Ratan means "Nine Gems" after the nine ingredients...but there appear to be ten...!

450 g (1 lb) cooking apples
450 g (1 lb) sugar
1 tsp onion seed
4 garlic cloves, finely chopped
2.5 cm (1") fresh ginger, finely chopped
1 tsp red chilli, finely chopped (or use chilli flakes)
2 tbsp freshly chopped mint (or 2 tsp dried)
225 ml (8 fl oz) vinegar – malt is best, but white vinegar works well too
1 tbsp raisins
1 tsp salt

1. Wash, peel, core and slice the apples; place in a saucepan with the sugar and 1 tbsp water; bring to the boil and simmer until the apples are soft.

2. Mash the apples with a hand masher and lower the heat to a minimum.

3. Add all the other ingredients and mix well together.

4. Pour while still hot into warm, sterilised jars, seal, cool and label.

Variations
Use gooseberries, topped and tailed, instead of apples.
Use raw mango – not ripe – instead of apples.

Raspberry Coulis

350 g (12 oz) fresh or frozen raspberries
6 tsp water
6 tsp caster sugar

FOOD, DRINK AND A FEW BITS MORE

1. Throw everything in the blender, whiz around for a few seconds, then sieve into a saucepan.

2. Boil for one minute, then cool and refrigerate.

Variation
Use blackberries instead of raspberries.

Herbs

Reality Check: ♈ ♈ ☺☺ £- ♥

> ⓘ Did you know....? You can keep an aloe vera plant in your home for small emergencies like minor burns – just cut off a small section of leaf and apply the glutinous part to the burn.

No need for dedicated space in the garden if you don't have it – herbs can be grown on the windowsill, in a window box or in a tub on a patio or flat roof. Either raise from seed or buy plants from the garden centre (don't replant pots bought at the supermarket).

Herbs are my absolute passion. I love the look of them, the smell of them and the taste of them. Planning my herb garden was an absolute joy, and tending to it always comes first on my job list in advance of more pressing work.

Unlike the vegetable patch, which is generally a more regimented design in rows or blocks, I think you can be much more creative with herbs and provide a more naturalistic garden with a definite "cottagey" feel, with a profusion of foliage, flowers and seed heads.

If, like me, you use a lot of herbs – for cooking, making tea, adding to pot pourri, making natural medicines or cosmetics – then you will find not only a rewarding pastime in growing herbs but the means to save a great deal of money. A small packet of basil from the supermarket costs around 75p; a packet of basil seeds, from which you can grow many tens of plants, costs around £1.50. Similarly, buying peppermint (or other herbal) teabags can become expensive if you drink as much as I do, whereas a freshly brewed tisane will not only be significantly cheaper but will also taste better and retain all its natural goodness.

No Room for a Herb Garden?

No problem. Herbs grow extremely well in window boxes, patio tubs, hanging baskets and on a sunny windowsill. Alternatively, if you have a garden but no space for a dedicated herb garden, just add a few herbs in your flower borders or vegetable patch. You will find they not only do well, but also positively benefit other plants and crops by attracting pollinators and deterring predators (who appear not to like some of the pungent smells or oiliness of the leaves). See also Companion Planting (later).

Planning a Herb Garden

If you do just one thing: Grow your favourite herb, or selection of herbs.

Whether you have just a square metre or a much larger plot for your herbs, the main thing you need is to be able to get in among them regularly to harvest leaves, flowers and seeds, as well as keep the weeds at bay. You can be quite creative with the design, or just keep it simple.

In my last garden I had a small, triangular plot just outside the back door that was sunny and sheltered, to which I added some paving slabs in chequerboard style so that I could get in among the plants. As you do this you inevitably brush up against the herbs and even step on them, but this releases their wonderful aroma and generally doesn't do them any harm. In fact I always plant creeping versions of herbs – mints, thymes, chamomile, etc. – at the edges of the border specifically to enjoy the scent when I walk past or even mow.

In my current garden I have dedicated a greedy 10-metre diameter circle, divided into eight plots, for my chosen herbs; figure 1 below shows you the design I selected. There were lots of designs to choose from. Here are just a few:

Figure 1: Herb Circle (like mine).

FOOD, DRINK AND A FEW BITS MORE

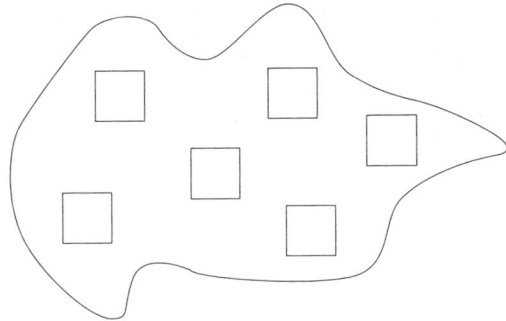

Figure 2: Freeform with stepping stones.

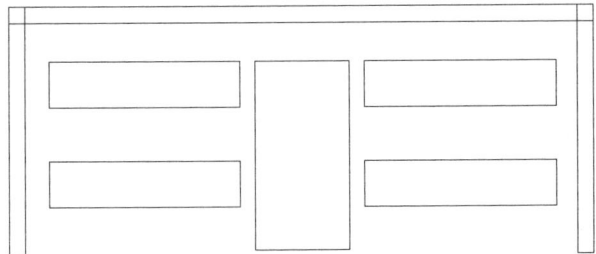

Figure 3: Formal, rectangular bed.

Planting Plan

Filling the herb plot can be done by choosing a theme:

- arranged by height, colour
- cosmetic herbs
- culinary herbs
- medicinal herbs
- pot pourri
- potager (block-filled areas, generally surrounded with a small hedge, e.g. box)
- teas and tisanes

I actually chose to use height as my theme because I am in such an exposed site I thought using some taller herbs (fennel, angelica, witch hazel, standard bay, lovage) around the outside might help to protect the inner plants from excessive wind. It partially works, but the poor tall plants do get a bit bombarded.

Grouping plants according to their intended use also works well – or have a different bed dedicated to a different theme. Take a look at the following table to help you decide.

HOW TO LIVE ON LESS

Herb	Height x Width	Culinary	Medicinal	Cosmetic/Home	Décoration	Tisane	Leaf	Stem	Flower	Fruit	Seed	Root
Angelica	8'x3'							•				•
Anise Hissop	2'6"x3'	•	•				•		•		•	
Basil	18"x12"	•			•	•	•					
Bay	3'x18"	•			•	•	•					
Bergamot	4'x18"						•					
Borage	24"x24"	•					•		•			
Caraway	24"x12"	•	•								•	
Chamomile	12"x12"					•			•			
Chervil	24"x12"	•					•					
Chives	12"x12"	•					•		•			
Comfrey	3'x3'		•				•					•
Coriander	24"x9"	•									•	
Curry plant	2'6"x3'				•		•					
Dill	5'x12"	•					•				•	•
Elecampane	8'x3'		•			•	•					
Fennel	7'x3'	•								•		
Feverfew	3'x12"		•									
Horseradish	3'x3'	•	•									
Juniper	20'x10'											
Lady's Mantle	2'x3'		•				•		•			
Lavender	24"x24"			•		•	•					
Lemon Balm	2'6"x18"		•			•	•					
Lemon Verbena	10'x5'											
Lovage	6'x3'	•					•					
Meadowsweet	3'x24"		•			•	•					
Mint	18"x18"	•				•	•					
Oregan•	3'x3'	•					•					
Parsley	24"x12"	•				•	•					
Purslane	18"x18"	•					•					
Rocket (wild)	18"x62	•					•					
Rose	3'x3'											
Rosemary	3'x3'	•				•	•					
Sage	3'x3'	•				•	•		•			
Salad Burnet	24"x12"	•					•					
Savory	12"x8"	•					•					
Sorrel (Buckler's)	18"x24"	•					•					
Sweet Cicely	3'x24"	•				•	•					
Sweet Marjoram	3'x3'	•					•					
Tarragon	2'6"x12"	•					•					
Thyme	24"x18"	•	•			•	•					
Yarrow	3'x12"		•			•	•					

FOOD, DRINK AND A FEW BITS MORE

Harvesting and Preserving Herbs

Herbs are at their best just before the flowering season and should be picked early in the morning before the heat of the sun gets to them. That way you'll get the full flavour of the herb's natural oils. Once picked, use the same day if you can, fresh in your chosen recipe, or preserve. Never pick more than one-third of the available leaf, so that the plant has the ability to regenerate.

Six of the Best: Practical methods for preserving herbs.

- **Drying**. Drying herbs intensifies the flavour, so when you eventually come to use the herb you will need less than the amount of fresh herb. I generally use my airing cupboard to dry my herbs. I stretch a cotton tea towel across a box and lay the herb over it, then leave for a couple of weeks, turning occasionally. When drying herbs, do one variety at a time. Don't mix them up, even if you intend to make pot pourri, as the flavours and scents will affect one another. Once dried, the leaves will be crisp and crumbly and can be stored in glass jars. Avoid the temptation of using clear glass and keeping your herbs on display – they will do much better in dark glass jars and kept in a cupboard.
- **Herbal Oil**. This is an excellent way of preserving fresh herb flavours that can then be used the whole year round. When I buy good quality olive oil, I buy a brand that has dark glass and a proper cork stopper: the bottles get reused all the time for herbal oil. Submerge a couple of handfuls of lightly-bruised fresh leaf in 600 ml (1 pint) light olive oil (not virgin or extra virgin – it's too strong) for culinary herbal oil, or almond oil for cosmetics, and leave on a sunny windowsill for a couple of weeks, shaking occasionally, but making sure the herbs remain submerged. (I always cover the leaves with a small plate to keep them below the oil.) Strain through muslin or a coffee filter to get a really clear liquid, bottle with a fresh sprig of herb, and label. If you prefer a stronger flavour or scent, repeat the process using fresh leaves.
  - If your herbal oil is for culinary purposes, experiment with either single herbs or a mixture of several herbal oils and add spices of your choice, e.g. coriander, fennel or dill seeds and/or fresh garlic and dried chillies that you've also grown in the kitchen garden, or cloves, mustard, allspice from the store cupboard.
  - If your herbal oil is for cosmetic purposes, use to massage into the skin as a conditioner or to relieve aches and pains.
- **Herbal Vinegar**. As for herbal oil, but use white wine or cider vinegar instead of oil. Do not use a metal seal for the bottle, as vinegar is corrosive.

- **Syrup.** Infuse several handfuls of fresh herbs in boiling water for 10 minutes, then strain. Add 450 g (1 lb) sugar to every 600 ml (1 pint) fluid and heat gently until the sugar is dissolved. Pour into clean, sterilised bottles, cool, seal and label.
- **Butter.** Finely chop 2 tbsp herbs and mash with 125 g (4 oz) unsalted butter. If you like, add finely chopped garlic and/or 1 tbsp lemon juice. Press into a rectangle or roll into a sausage, then pack in greaseproof paper. Keeps in the fridge for a few days, or can be frozen for up to one month, in which case cut into rounds and place greaseproof paper between the portions.
- **Freezing.** Unlike drying, freezing reduces the flavour of herbs, but it is nevertheless a practical method for preserving them. Chop individual herbs finely and pack into ice cube trays. Fill with water and freeze. To use, just pop a few herbal ice cubes into your recipe. Borage flowers can be frozen whole in this way to add to Pimms in the summer.

Using Herbs

> ⓘ Did you know...? Comfrey mixed with water makes a very quick and effective (but oh, so smelly) natural fertiliser. Alternatively you can place it directly onto the compost heap to speed up decomposition.

Fresh

Nothing tastes better than the addition of some fresh herbs into your cooking, and their specific flavours generally obviate the need to add salt, so help to ensure you eat healthily. Robust herbs such as rosemary, sage and thyme can be added during the cooking process – whether a slow-cooked casserole or roasted meat or vegetables – whereas more delicate herbs such as coriander, basil and chervil are better thrown in or over right at the end.

Fresh herbs can transform some otherwise mundane base products and turn them into something really delicious. Add some finely chopped herbs to mayonnaise or yoghurt to provide a quick and tasty dip or salad dressing; the classic "fines herbes" combination of parsley, chives, tarragon and chervil transform a plain omelette into fast food extraordinaire; and blitzing herbs in a pestle or liquidiser with nuts, garlic and oil creates a tasty "pesto" which can transform any number of dishes (see recipe).

FOOD, DRINK AND A FEW BITS MORE

Heating herbs either by adding them to hot water or throwing into a fire encourages them to release their natural oils and as such they can be used to gently scent and flavour anything that is steamed over herb-infused water or barbecued over coals liberally sprinkled with herbs. If left to steep in hot water for about five minutes, several herbs like rosemary, sage, mint, lemon verbena and chamomile make a very acceptable tea with mild therapeutic properties.

Dried
From a culinary perspective I think dried herbs rate a poor second to fresh, but they are invaluable during the winter months when fresh herbs may not be available. The strength of the herb increases during the drying process, and typically when 2 tbsp fresh herbs are specified only 2 tsp dried herbs are needed.

We can use this increased strength to our advantage in non-culinary uses. For example, pot pourri uses a range of dried herbs together with dried citrus peel, pine cones, cinnamon, etc. to make a pleasantly scented dried dish to gently fragrance the room. Other dried herbs have a scent that repels pests (see the sections on Natural Pest Control). The scent released from the oil when hot water is poured over herbs becomes an effective mood enhancer, thus dried herbs work well in a muslin bag hung under the hot water tap of the bath, or in facial steams and therapeutic foot baths.

A range of interesting teas and tisanes can also be made from dried herbs – like culinary herbs, use less of the dried version.

Oil
Use for: dressing salads, roasting vegetables or meat, adding to bread; chilli and garlic oil is particularly good poured over pizza just before eating.

Vinegar
Use for marinades, salad dressings and hair rinses.

Syrup
Use undiluted to flavour cakes and sweet dishes, or diluted to make into drinks.

HOW TO LIVE ON LESS

Herbal Recipes

Sweet Cicely Polish
Pound fresh, soft sweet cicely seeds in a mortar. Pick up a handful in a cloth and rub on wood as a polish.

Crystallised Angelica
Really, really easy…but it takes such a long time! Do persevere, as the end result is worth it!

1 kg (2¼lb) granulated sugar
425 ml (14 fl oz) water
Angelica stalks

1. Wash and peel the angelica stalks and cut into short lengths – about 10 cm (4") long.

2. Soak overnight in cold water to clean and soften, then drain the angelica.

3. In a large pan, dissolve the sugar in the water and bring to the boil.

4. Add the drained angelica and boil for 5 minutes.

5. Use a slotted spoon to remove the angelica and place on a cake rack over a drip tray to dry. Any drips can be added back to the sugar solution in the pan.

6. Repeat this process twice a day for four days. The layer of sugar crystals will gradually build up and the angelica will become softer.

Keep any crystallised sugar from the pan for use in cakes.

Store crystallised angelica in airtight jars and use in cake making and puddings.

Pesto
The word "pesto" simply means "pounded" – it does not have to be based on the traditional ingredients of basil or pine nuts. I have a couple of mature walnut trees and an extensive herb garden, so pesto is regularly on our menu.

FOOD, DRINK AND A FEW BITS MORE

Ingredients
75 g (2¾ oz) nuts – select a single type, e.g. walnuts, pine nuts, hazelnuts, cob nuts.
2 cloves garlic
1 tsp salt
2 large handfuls fresh herb – select a single type, e.g. basil, coriander, parsley, rocket
100 ml (3½ fl oz) extra virgin olive oil

Method
1. Mince the nuts, garlic and herbs and pound with the salt. You can do this in a pestle and mortar or a food processor. I prefer to end up with a mixture that still has texture and visible bits of nut and garlic, but you can choose to make a smooth paste if you prefer.

2. Add the oil a little at a time until you have a thick paste.

Uses
- Spread thickly over one side of a fish or meat steak, or top tomatoes or mushrooms, and bake or grill.
- Use to dress pasta.
- Drizzle over salads – you can thin with additional olive oil to make it more runny.
- Add a dollop to a vegetable soup before serving.
- Use in sandwiches instead of mayonnaise.
- Combine with mayonnaise and/or yoghurt to make an instant dip for crudités.

Cut Flower Garden

Reality Check: 🍸🍸 ☺☺ ££- £+ ❤

My girlfriend Linda has been growing flowers for cutting for many, many years. Although her north London garden is not large, she grows the plants she simply adores and is completely self-sufficient in cut flowers from about March through to September. All of the flowers she grows are native, and they are truly splendid: she gets some amazing three-headed gladioli, the huge pompoms on some of her chrysanthemums are to die for, and somehow the faces on her daffodils just seem much bigger than mine, or perhaps more striking. I asked her what her secret was. The only thing she could think of was that she had purposefully chosen her stock from a

Dutch supplier, believing that they may have superior quality than the average British garden centre.

Linda has organised her garden into generous clumps of the same plant, so that even when numerous stalks are cut for taking inside or for gifting to friends, there is still always plenty on display in the garden. Also, it means she has a stock of plants that will provide seeds for collecting, drying and sowing next year. Her front garden is home to night-scented stocks and old roses that additionally provide a welcoming scent as you come and go from the house. Organising flowers to provide outdoor interest as well as being able to cut them for indoor display might be an important consideration for you, too. Otherwise, and particularly if you have a large area that can be dedicated to a cut flower garden, you might choose to follow the commercial growers' format of having long rows of the same plant so that you can provide the support each needs and get between them for weeding and harvesting.

What to Grow
What you choose to grow is completely personal – it depends on what you like to have in your garden and what you like to have in your vase. Some plants are soil-specific, e.g. rhododendrons thrive on acid soil, so a little bit of homework will help before you get started. In this table I've provided you with some ideas of what flowers are good for cutting and the season when they will be at their best. Don't forget to include foliage in your plans – as well as being attractive in its own right, it provides a useful foil and contrast to display flowers at their best.

Cutting and Conditioning

> ① Did you know...? Viagra is good for doubling the vase life of cut flowers, making them stand up straight for as long as a week beyond their natural lifespan. Use ½ mg per vase (as opposed to 50 mg for men).

When you cut a flower stalk, or some foliage, you are effectively removing its life support system, and from that moment on the cut plant is susceptible to the environment. Roses are particularly sensitive. You need to treat your plants with respect and provide the right care, so that they reward you with a long and healthy vase life.

FOOD, DRINK AND A FEW BITS MORE

Spring	Summer		Autumn	Winter
Daffodil	Acanthus	Honesty (flower)	Anemone	Cornus (coloured bark)
Euphorbia	Achillea	Lavender	Chrysanthemum	
Gaura (catkins)	Ageratum	Lilly	Dahlia	Holly
Hellebore	Antirrhinum	Lupin	Eremurus	Ivy
Lily of the valley	Allium	Love-in-a-mist	Fern (foliage)	Mistletoe
Solomon's seal	Aster	Peony	Helenium	Willow (coloured bark)
Spiraea	Azalea	Philadelphus (foliage)	Honesty (seed pod)	
Tulip	Calendula	Poppy (flower)	Nerine	
Viburnum	Campanula	Ranunculus	Poppy (seed head)	
Willow (catkins)	Cerinthe	Rhododendron	Rudbeckia	
	Cleome	Rose	Sedum	
	Cornflower	Salvia	Teasel	
	Cosmos	Scabious	Yarrow (seed head)	
	Dianthus	Stock		
	Dill (foliage)	Sunflower		
	Fennel (foliage)	Sweet pea		
	Freesia	Sweet William		
	Foxglove	Tagetes		
	Gaura (foliage)	Yarrow (flower)		
	Gladiolus	Zinnia		
	Gypsophila			

Six of the Best: Practical tips for keeping your cut flowers looking their best.

- Take a bucket of water with you on your cutting trip so that the cut stems go straight into water and get an immediate drink (this should additionally help to stop any air locks in the stem, which is often the cause of wilting). Use warm water for most plants; cold water for bulb flowers (warm water will accelerate the flowers opening).
- Pick flowers early in the day before the heat of the sun gets to them, or in the cool of the evening; these are the times when the stems have the maximum amount of water in them.
- Use a sharp pair of scissors or secateurs to cut the stems – on no account should you just yank the stem from its parent, as crushing or damaging the stems in any way will shorten their vase life.
- When ready to put into a vase, make a diagonal cut across the stem at your chosen height.
- Take off any foliage that will be below the water level, otherwise the foliage will decay and form bacteria that will clog the stem ends, preventing uptake of water (not to mention making the water smell nasty!).
- Put the flowers in a clean vase with fresh water to which plant food has been added and refresh the water after a few days; during the ensuing days and weeks deadhead (snip off rather than pull) any dead, diseased or dying flowers, or remove the flower completely from the vase.

There are also a number of specific actions you need to take with individual plants:

- Roses often enjoy having their stems re-cut after a few days to avoid wilting; this will unfortunately make the stems more susceptible to an air lock, so either place the cut end into near-boiling water to destroy the air lock and/or stick a pin through their heads.
- Don't put daffodils into water with anything else, as they exude a poisonous substance that will kill other flowers.
- If tulips need to be kept waiting before they get to a vase, wrap them reasonably tightly in newspaper to keep their stems from bending over, and leave upright in water.
- Anything with a woody stem like azalea, lilac or rhododendron should have all foliage removed as it prevents water reaching the flower head.
- Don't cut dianthus (pinks) across their knobbly knees – cut across the straight part of the stem.
- I always remove the stamen from lilies because I have a pale carpet and they can create quite a nasty stain.
- The bottom of the stem of some bulb flowers curl at the end – snip off the curl and change the water.

Natural Pest Control (Outdoors)
We can all learn to tolerate a number of pests in the interest of organic gardening and biodiversity; however, infestations of black fly, slugs and snails, ants, etc. are upsetting to humans and potentially devastating to crops.

There are numerous natural methods that we can use to control pests, taking a more holistic approach to organic gardening, without resorting to commercial chemicals that are costly and, worse still, will eventually end up inside us. The most notable natural pest control is to have really good soil to promote strong and healthy growth. After that, try the following:

- Companion Planting
- Natural Deterrents and Barriers
- Wildlife

FOOD, DRINK AND A FEW BITS MORE

Companion Planting

Reality Check: ⚐ ⚐ ☺☺ ££- ♥

Companion planting is about deliberately placing plants together that can benefit each other in some way. In some examples you may actually want both crops – for example, growing carrots and onions together appears to confuse the harmful flies which would otherwise attack each crop; in other examples, the "companion" may actually be sacrificial as predators eat or infect the plant but leave the target crop alone. The subject of companion planting is actually much wider than natural pest control – for example, plants like sweet corn, if grown in a block, provide natural shelter to anything grown behind it; other plants change the soil by adding/removing elements or, like potatoes, improving the whole structure of the lower soil at the same time as providing very good ground cover and weed suppression.

In terms of natural pest control, companion planting can work in the following ways:

- Some plants are good at luring pests away from more susceptible hosts by confusing the pests with their strong scent, sometimes sacrificing their own lives for the greater good of your crop. Strong-smelling plants like garlic, shallots and pungent herbs appear to reduce the amount of aphids; chives planted under apple trees help protect them against scab; basil is the classic companion for tomatoes; and nasturtiums are supposed to be beneficial for beans, as they attract bees for pollination and lure away the black fly from the bean crop (though all I got last year was a bumper crop of nasturtiums!).
- Other plants may attract beneficial insects onto your crops – for example, bees for pollination or ladybirds to eat aphids. Planting sweet peas with beans attracts bees at the right time of year. I have a number of golden oregano bushes that are always teaming with bees; there's one next to my front door, and as you walk past the bees lift a few inches and buzz a little louder as if in farewell or greeting. The poached egg plant, Limnanthes douglasii, grown under gooseberry and blackcurrant bushes will allegedly increase the crop by attracting and feeding beneficial insects – frankly, anything that will increase my measly crop of two blackcurrants would be welcome, though perhaps time and good pruning are also factors here!

- Plants may also attract birds onto your plot that prey on pests. Birds themselves also do some damage, but on balance I think they are more beneficial than harmful. We have moorhens on our pond and they seem to do a good job keeping down the slugs and snails.
- Attractive plants bring joy to humans too, so that we are encouraged to go to the plot and/or spend more time there.

Natural Deterrents and Barriers

Reality Check: ȲȲ ①① ££- ♥

My plot backs onto a field full of wild rabbits. They quickly turned from being cute little white-tailed bunnies hopping freely around my garden to the most hated of pests, devouring all the plants and shrubs in the border and digging out newly-planted trees to nibble the wood below the surface. We put up a rabbit wire fence all around the perimeter – it was dug 30 cm into the ground and was 90 cm tall. The rabbits jumped over it, squealing with delight at the new toy their favourite food providers had just erected for them. So we raised the fence by another 30cm and I have to say it was fun for us to watch them as they failed to clear the height but bounced back off the wire. So, instead, they got themselves organised, and now they tunnel under the fence...

I guess the rabbits are still our primary pest, but as our plot matures, the amount of damage that the one or two that do get in are capable of doing is significantly reduced. I now know that I need to protect my campanulas, hebes and hollies – the rest is fair game. We have been lucky, so far, with other types of pests but hopefully that's because we've put the right kind of companion planting in and have managed to attract a number of allies – moorhens, ducks, owls, a variety of birds, ladybirds, lacewings, etc. – that keep the pest population to a controllable level.

Your garden will no doubt have its own annoying set of pests. You just need to find a way around it, or get it to a level, like us and our rabbit population, where it's manageable and the damage acceptable.

> Six of the Best: Practical ideas for keeping your garden pests at bay.
>
> - **Barrier.** Erect a physical barrier to keep pests off carrots, rabbits out of gardens, birds and mammals away from fruit and vulnerable stems. Options to achieve a barrier include rabbit wire, fruit cage,

FOOD, DRINK AND A FEW BITS MORE

fleece stretched over hoops to make a mini-polytunnel, plastic stem guards, egg shells or copper piping around plants to deter slugs.
- **Cover.** Use cloches (which you can make by cutting the bottom off plastic bottles) to cover vulnerable seedlings, horticultural fleece to cover fruit bushes when fruiting.
- **Removal.** Just use your fingers to pull insects off plants, or pick out the top of the plant or individual leaves that seem to be attracting the most pests.
- **Scarer.** Erect a string of CDs between two canes and site over any crops that you want to keep the birds off; use a scarecrow – reuse for Guy Fawkes.
- **Spray.** Aim a jet of water at any crop that has a pest infestation; if they are particularly stubborn, use a water spray with a little washing-up liquid added.
- **Trap.** Sink a plastic cup (or bottle bottom) into the ground and fill with beer to trap slugs; soak strips of fabric or masking tape in a sugar solution to make fly and wasp traps.

Wildlife

Attracting beneficial wildlife into our gardens gives us the pleasure of seeing the birds, mammals, invertebrates, etc. in the garden, as well as the added bonus that many actually improve the garden by keeping pests in check. It's a difficult balance, however, making sure we have the right habitat to attract such natural allies and provide the right food and accommodation to allow them to feed, breed and shelter.

Using the Food Chain to Keep Pests in Check

Reality Check: ♈ ☉ £- ♥

The following table will give you some ideas about the most common types of wildlife that are a benefit to the organic kitchen garden, and some simple food and habitat measures you can take to attract and retain them.

Wildlife	Benefit to Garden	Food to Attract	Habitat to Retain
Bees	Pollinate plants. Blue and great tits, robins, wrens, house sparrows and blackbirds depend on huge quantities of grubs for their chicks.	Pollen and nectar - provide a variety of trees, plants, shrubs that flower at different times of the year (with flower structures that allow the bee to get in).	Dead wood - drill small holes for them to get into; trees, shrubs, flowering plants.

HOW TO LIVE ON LESS

Wildlife	Benefit to Garden	Food to Attract	Habitat to Retain
Birds	Adult birds such as house sparrows, tits and chaffinches feed on aphids and other insects. Blackbirds and thrushes eat slugs and snails. Blackbirds eat worms and spiders. Robins feed on small soil invertebrates.	Trees, flowers, shrubs all supply insects, fruits, seeds that birds will eat. Blackbirds eat cotoneaster berries. Finches and tits feed on seed heads - fennel, teasel, thistle, golden rod, sunflowers. Birds use tree canopy for shelter and nests. Put out seeds, nuts, fruit, fat blocks in bird feeders or on a table; add a bird bath.	Thick leafy climbers, mature trees, shrubs, hedgerow. Nesting boxes.
Devil's coach-horse beetles	Feed on different types of invertebrate, particularly wine weevils.		Ground-cover plants and plant litter - dark, moist conditions.
Frogs, toads, newts	Eat slugs.	Pond life.	Pond (or just a waterproof vessel sunk into the ground, filled with water); Pile of logs and sticks; ground-cover plants.
Hedgehogs	Eat slugs, snails, caterpillars, beetles, worms.	Meat-based pet food and cat biscuits.	Pile of logs and sticks; compost; thick piles of dead leaves.
Ground beetles	Eat slugs, snails and other soil-living creatures.		Dead wood - just leave a pile of wood in a corner.
Hoverflies	Larvae eat aphids - one hoverfly larva can devour around 1,000 aphids in its lifetime.	Pollen and nectar, especially angelica, coriander, fennel.	Pile of logs and sticks; long grass.
Lacewings	Larvae eat aphids; adults eat greenfly, whitefly, red spider mites to name but a few.		Bundled hollow canes and plant stems; long grass.
Ladybirds	Adults and larvae eat aphids, greenfly, black fly.		Bundled hollow canes and plant stems; leaf litter.
Spiders	Eat aphids and flying pests.		Pile of logs and sticks; any nook or cranny.
Tachinid flies	Eat caterpillars and other grubs.		
Wasps	Eat aphids, caterpillars and flies.		

FOOD, DRINK AND A FEW BITS MORE

Compost Contents

The Right Things
The key to good compost is to get the balance right. You need both brown, woody, fibrous material (carbon-rich), mixed with green, wet, soft material (nitrogen-rich), approximately in the ratio four parts woody to one part green. I usually spend a week throwing my kitchen and household waste on the compost, which makes one layer, and then all the prunings, clippings, deadheads etc. from the week in the garden get added as the next layer, with an occasional wheelbarrowful of grass cuttings. Last birthday my friend Richard and his daughter Grace gifted me four big bagfuls of horse manure – produced locally by their own horse – which came not only as a wonderful surprise and a much-appreciated gift but also a most welcome addition to the compost. And, of course, this is a really good example of self-sufficiency at its best – they have more manure than they know what to do with, and for me it's like gold dust! I do hope I get some more... If you keep chickens or pigs, their manure is also a good addition to the compost heap. Aim for a final compost pile of about three feet high.

Collecting organic kitchen waste is easy and you'll be surprised just how quickly it mounts up. I keep a huge crockery bowl on my worktop – purchased many years ago to make Christmas puddings and only used once – into which I drop scraps as they are created. They include tea bags, vegetable peelings, banana skins, bits of raw fruit and vegetables that have passed their best, coffee dregs, etc. Despite the fact that citrus fruit is organic, collective wisdom suggests you shouldn't put too much orange and lemon peel onto the compost – I generally limit mine to the half-lemon I squeeze each morning but avoid the 5–6 oranges we squeeze when making juice. It usually only takes two days to fill the bowl, so there's never any problem with smell or decay. Of course, you could have your kitchen waste collector in a cupboard next to the bin, or even outside the back door, but in my house it's out of sight, out of mind, and I would forget to use it if it wasn't right in front of me.

Household waste doesn't get generated quite so quickly, but when it does it goes straight on the compost heap. I have a paper shredder in my office and I regularly shred paper (an occupational hazard!), but I also use it to shred cardboard boxes. All my empty cereal boxes go through very nicely and that means I don't have to tear them up into little bits. I used to shred all the newspapers as well, but now I prefer to soak them in water then put round both sides of the perimeter fence, covered with grass clippings, as a natural weed suppressor. Other household waste items that can go on the compost heap include the contents of the vacuum cleaner, ash from the wood-burning stove, kitchen towel, paper hankies and fluff from the tumble drier. Clothing or bags made entirely from natural fibres – cotton, linen, hessian, jute, wool, silk – can also go on the compost heap but need to be cut into tiny pieces first: you wouldn't want to dig over your plot and find that old sock again!

> ⓘ Did you know...? Nitrogen-rich plants like stinging nettles and comfrey make a very effective natural accelerator for the compost. During the course of the year I cut back the stinging nettles that surround my plot to add to the pile, plus I grow comfrey in a dedicated bin to provide a quick-boost layer to the compost and to make liquid fertiliser.

The Wrong Things
Do not add any cooked foods to the compost as it may attract vermin. Nor for the same reason should you add meat or fish, whether raw or cooked. Non-organic material such as glass, plastic, metal, crockery etc. should not be added even if there is a symbol suggesting that it is biodegradable. The home compost is not suitable for such items as it doesn't generate sufficient heat to break down their structures. They should be recycled as directed by your local council. From the garden, do not add wood unless you can shred it reasonably finely, and keep your leaves separate from the compost for making leaf mould (see later). Leaves take a couple of years to rot fully, and make a useful soil improver in their own right. At the end of the growing season do not add seed heads, as these may stay viable in the compost for a very long time unless there is sufficient heat to destroy them. Finally, I don't like to add too many grass cuttings, because the pile gets too slimy.

Decomposition
As mentioned above, the compost heap does need heat, moisture and air to perform its magic. As you create new layers of waste, always add some moisture – I keep the water I use to cook pasta and potatoes (because I don't like to add those to the stock pot) and the dregs from the coffee machine, plus I swish out the huge bowl I keep the kitchen waste in with water from the pond and throw that onto the pile. I know that some people add urine – and a very nutritious addition it is too – but I've not done that yet. Air can be added by occasionally digging over the heap. You will see over time that the level of the compost drops as it compacts, so just get the garden fork in and turn it over. If you have several compost

bins, then you can fork from one into another. Finally, to add heat, cover the compost heap either with a purpose-built lid or, like me, with a layer of spare carpet; we have plenty lying around in the attic waiting for just such a purpose.

In theory, then, making your own compost should be reasonably straightforward so long as you get the balance right. My friends Chris and Carme, who live just outside Barcelona, had an amusing experience with theirs. They had been given some compost from a non-commercial source and decided to add a nice thick layer all over their garden. Next month they saw seedlings popping up all across the garden – nothing that Chris had ever planted – and within a couple of months they had a garden full of tomatoes of all different varieties. You can imagine under the glorious Spanish sun how these plants flourished! He and his son kept them well watered, but just couldn't keep on top of the harvest, let alone find willing friends and neighbours to take the produce and to take over the watering and harvest while they visited their friends and family in the UK.

Leaf Mould
If you have trees either in the garden or around the house, you'll know just how many leaves there are to collect in the autumn. Rather than putting them into the bin, why not make leaf mould? It's simple to do but takes a little time for the leaves to decompose into something useful. For this reason, I don't put very many leaves onto the compost heap – they don't decay as rapidly as other elements, so are best left on their own.

As you sweep up the leaves, place them into a plastic gardening or refuse bag. If they're not already wet, add some water so that the decomposition process can start. Pierce some holes in the bag so that air can freely circulate, then leave for a minimum of one year but better two before you use. Check from time to time that the leaves haven't dried out, and add some water if they have. After one year the leaf mould makes reasonable mulch. After two years when the mould is more mature it makes a very useful soil improver. And all for free.

Beverages

Only recently have I discovered how delicious, varied and refreshing home-made fruit and vegetable juices can be. I took the decision to try these out when a few extra grams around my midriff turned into a few extra kilos and thus required an amendment to my usual diet. Now I count carrot-and-beetroot juice and cucumber-with-lemon-grass among my favourite daily treats. Then, with a change to my daily work routine that resulted in more time at home, came the decision to start my own kitchen garden. What other people were calling "surplus" from their vegetable patch, I started to look upon as fresh juice. Friends and family have since enlightened me to the fact that the same raw ingredients make the most acceptable country-style wines or alcoholic beverages and so started, or maybe rekindled, an interest in home-made wines, beers and spirits. All to the detriment once again of my waistline, I might add, but then I guess there's always the gym…

Home-Brewed Beer

Reality Check: ΥΥ ☺☺☺ ££-

Brewing, like wine-making, is basically a process of making an alcoholic drink by the fermentation by yeast of a flavoured, sugary solution. In the case of beer, the sugary solution is a malt solution flavoured with hops. When yeast, a living organism, is added to the hopped malt solution, it "feeds" on the sugar to obtain the energy it needs for self-reproduction, and the by-products of the reproductive process are carbon dioxide and alcohol. Carbon dioxide provides the beer's sparkle and head. Alcohol-wise, you should get a final beer strength of anything between 3% and 6%.

The Brewing Process

For many of us, home brewing starts life with a beer-making kit of some kind. For my friend Richard, this meant a mini-brewery called a BrewZer from the Miracle Beer Company, which simply requires ten minutes to add water to a powder and then two weeks' wait until the beer is ready to drink. My husband, his brother and their father have all been avid home brewers using the more conventional beer-making kit where you buy extract malt and use a five-gallon plastic fermenting bin – I dare say many of you will have such bins still lying around the attic somewhere. I'll tell you a bit more about each brewing-kit method later in this section, but

FOOD, DRINK AND A FEW BITS MORE

either way, these beer-making kits provide perfectly acceptable results with the minimum amount of expenditure on equipment and the minimum amount of fuss.

However, the more serious home brewer wants to be able to customise his brew and get involved in the whole process.

I have therefore described below how to make beer from first principles, identifying the points in the process at which short cuts can be made, either from purchasing specific ingredients or using a beer-making kit.

Equipment
Large vessel in which to mash grains
Boiling pan
A wide-necked straining bag or sieve
5-gallon polythene dustbin
Thermometer
Hydrometer
Spray
40 pint bottles with seal and labels, or five 1-gallon glass jars, or a barrel

Ingredients
Barley grain
Hops or other herbs (dandelion, burdock, nettle, ginger)
Other grains: maize, rice, wheat
Invert sugar
Yeast
Water

Method
Malting
Malting consists of inducing the grain to produce enzymes that modify the starch, in which the plant has stored energy, so that it can be converted into sugars that the beer yeast can feed on. The process is then halted by heating the malt and reducing it to "grist" by lightly crushing it.

- Malting of barley grain is a tricky process to achieve successfully at home and is the first part of the brewing process that can be bypassed by purchasing ready-kilned malt.

Mashing

Mashing converts the starch in the grist to maltose and extracts it. This is achieved by simmering a porridge of grist and water at a constant temperature of around 64°C (150°F) for about 2-2½ hours. Different temperatures result in different proportions of malt sugars (maltose, sucrose and dextrin) – the closer to 60°C, the more maltose; the closer to 70°C, the more dextrin – and this will affect the character of the beer.

The iodine test is an easy and foolproof test for checking to see whether the conversion to maltose has completed (essential for your beer to be clear rather than hazy). Put a tablespoon of malt solution onto some white porcelain – a cup, a saucer or a tile work well – then add a few drops of tincture of iodine. If there is starch still present in the mash, the colour darkens or goes blue, in which case maintain the temperature under the mash for another half hour, then repeat the test. If the solution remains unchanged, the mashing process is complete.

Sparging

The mash is now strained to draw off the sugar-laden liquid (the "wort") into a boiling pan. The remaining mash is "sparged" – a process by which hot water is sprayed over the mash to wash the last of the sugars out of the grain – and the left-over grains discarded.

- The home brewer can bypass the malting, mashing and sparging processes by purchasing malt sugars already extracted from the grain malt. Malt extract can be bought as a sticky syrup in various grades or malt extract powder.

Boiling

The wort, whether from malt grain or from powdered or syrup malt extract is then boiled up with the hops for about an hour to extract their bitter flavour and to prevent deterioration and help the beer clear rapidly. You will need between 10–40 g (½–1½ oz) of hops per gallon. Copper finings or Irish moss may also be added at this stage to help reduce the risk of hazing – these coagulate unwanted proteins that then sink to the bottom of the beer. At the end of boiling, leave the vessel for half an hour while the hops and any sediment settle. Additional hops may be added when the beer is finally kegged, a process known as "dry-hopping" which adds extra tanginess to the flavour.

FOOD, DRINK AND A FEW BITS MORE

- What you now have is a hopped malt solution, and the remaining beer-making process is the same as the one used by traditional beer-making kits.

Fermentation
The hopped malt solution is now strained from the hops into a fermentation vessel, the sugar added and the vessel topped up with cold water. When it has cooled to about 16°C, pitch the yeast.

Sprinkle yeast onto the surface but don't stir it in – yeast is a living organism that needs oxygen in order to function. Cover the vessel loosely and leave it somewhere that can be kept at a constant temperature of 18–24°C (65–75°F). After about 24 hours you should see the first signs that the brew is fermenting, and after a day or so the yeast will have thrown up a frothy head: skim this off. On the second and third days "rouse" (stir) the beer. Full fermentation takes around 5–7 days, after which bubbles stop rising and the specific gravity measures 1.010 or below. Move the beer to a cool place for another couple of days to let it stand and clear, ready for bottling or casking.

Siphoning and Bottling
Prime the beer by stirring 50 g (1¾ oz) sugar dissolved in a little warm water into the beer (or alternatively put ½ tsp sugar in each bottle). Keep the suction end of the siphon above the sediment at the bottom of the fermenting vessel and rack (siphon) the beer off carefully into the bottles or jars, leaving 4 cm (1½ in) at the top of each bottle to allow space for the build up of pressure. Store in a warm place for 3–4 days to get the secondary fermentation going, then move to a cool store for a week or two while the beer matures.

Casking
Beer may be casked instead of bottled, which may add a bit more cost up-front but saves significantly on the labour involved in bottling. Kegged beer takes longer to mature than bottled beer, but has the advantage that you can draw off a smaller (or larger!) quantity whenever you want.

The first few pints will flow easily from the tap, in good condition and full of life. After that, carbon dioxide from the second fermentation fills the gap and prevents air being drawn in. The carbon dioxide must either be released using an injector bulb fitted to the lid, or a second priming using 25 g (1 oz) sugar is needed.

HOW TO LIVE ON LESS

Beer-Making Kits

Standard Home-Brew Kits

There are numerous home-brew kits on the market, many available online, supplying everything you need, except water and a can opener. These are the products that my husband was brought up on, and they make a very good pint of beer. For around £50 you can purchase all the equipment and ingredients you need to brew and bottle 30–40 pints (18–25 litres) of beer (somehow I can't bring myself to put the metric version first, as I have throughout this book – beer is quite simply measured by the pint, or half pint!). Once you're set up with the equipment, refill cans of all styles of beer are available, again online, starting from around £8 for 40 pints of basic bitter – that's just 20p per pint, a significant saving over pub bitter which currently costs from £2.80 per pint.

Mini-Home-Brewery

Reality Check: Ƴ ☉ ££-

Somewhat newer to the home-brew market are the mini-home-breweries. They take advantage of new technologies and dried ingredients for making beer. As the name suggests, mini-home-breweries produce smaller quantities of beer, but are an ideal place to start out.

Like many of us, my friend Richard likes a few beers in the pub now and again, but was sufficiently impressed by the quality of the beer from the BrewZer mini-brewery system he was gifted to want to go ahead and buy some refills.

BrewZer, by the Miracle Beer Company, is a self-contained mini-10-pint brewery that's easy to set up at home. It uses all natural products – East Anglian barley, hops and brewer's yeast – which have been blended into a powder to which you just add tap water. Once mixed, fermentation takes place in the BrewZer pressure-controlled brewing vessel, which also helps clarify the beer. Once you've assembled the mini-brewery, it only takes 10 minutes to mix the ingredients with water and set up the brewery, and then 14 days to wait until the beer's ready to drink.

What you end up with is an old-fashioned-style, strong living beer – bitter, lager, IPA or stout – which is stronger than the average pub bitter (4.5%

FOOD, DRINK AND A FEW BITS MORE

ABV), with a light head and a fizz-free body. If you actually prefer to have a more fizzy beer, there are instructions with the pack to increase carbonation by adding sugar, thus encouraging a second fermentation in the bottle. The carbonated beer is best drunk within two weeks of bottling.

It will cost you £32.99 to get started with a BrewZer mini-brewery, for which you get a reusable barrel, lid assembly and pump, and a ten-pint starter pack of Miracle Beer powder with disposable sterilised components. This means that your first ten pints of Miracle Beer will cost you £3.30 per pint – marginally more expensive than pub beer. 30-pint refills are available online at £29.99 (or 10-pint refills for £14.99) and are provided complete with their own pre-sterilised components – the beer tube, tap, liner, valves, etc. – so follow-on pints of beer will cost you just £1. With pub bitter at £2.80 a pint, that's quite a big saving! See www.one2brew.com or www.happybrewer.co.uk.

Making Country-Style Wines

Reality Check: ⚘ ⚘ ☺☺☺ ££-

If you glance through the recipes in any home wine-making book, you will notice that there are as many ways to make wine as there are base ingredients to make it from. And on the face of it, quite a lot of equipment too. But actually, I think the basics of wine-making – fermenting a sugar-rich, flavoured liquid – are quite straightforward, and the amount of kit you purchase can be minimised…until, that is, you get the bug! And that's where the fun begins. Because, as I've just said, all you're doing is taking some tasty liquid, loading it with sugar, and fermenting it. The process becomes more sophisticated when you want to reduce haze or sweetness or increase flavour.

You can experiment with just about any ingredient to get new and unusual flavours, exciting blends or an improved colour – fruit and vegetables (fresh, frozen, dried, tinned), flowers, leaves, herbs, sap and tea all have the potential to be your base flavours, either on their own or mixed together. Specific plants to avoid in wine-making include bluebells, buttercups, daffodils, ivy, rhubarb leaves, laburnum, unripe (green) potatoes and yew. Otherwise, any of your garden produce and even the hedgerow can be turned very easily into a delicious, home-made alcoholic drink with the addition of a few specialist products and perhaps with a few items from your store cupboard. Just add new ingredients when you want

– rose petals, more tannin (using a cup tea), cloves, sultanas, etc. Experiment and have fun; there are no hard-and-fast rules.

As for method, once you have your liquid, it's pretty similar for all recipes. But how you get your liquid differs from ingredient to ingredient, depending on whether it needs to be pulped, crushed, boiled or macerated in order to extract the most flavour and fluid. Think how easy it is to throw some sugar over sliced strawberries and watch them bleed out their juice. Now try the same idea with a parsnip. Doesn't work, does it? And yet parsnips, when the juice is properly prepared for fermenting, make the most delicious wine.

In the following pages I have attempted to simplify the wine-making process into four different initial methods so that you get an appreciation of how to extract juice and the different ingredients used in wine-making. However, if you are going to be a serious wine-maker, I urge you to purchase a decent recipe book and try whatever takes your fancy, whether it's because you simply love the idea of gooseberry wine or you have surplus root vegetables that you want to do something different with. As you experiment, note that flowers and leaves add bouquet and flavour in droves but don't provide good body, so they are generally added with other ingredients.

Equipment
Large capacity 10–12.5 litres (2–3 gallons) food-quality white polythene bin with lid (any other colour may leach)
5 litre (1 gallon) glass jars with stopper – demijohns – you will probably need several for fermentation and storage
Bored fermentation bung and airlock
Funnel
Spoon – long-handled polythene, not metal or wood
Siphon – plastic tubing about 1 m (3 ft) long and glass U-bend
Straining bag – nylon, cotton or calico or nylon sieve plus muslin
Hydrometer
Bottles and corks, labels
Record book and wine-making recipe books

Specialist Products and Other Ingredients

Acid	Citric (or malic, tartaric) acid needs to be added if there are insufficient quantities in your base product, as yeast will not ferment without acid; also helps to preserve wine.

FOOD, DRINK AND A FEW BITS MORE

Pectic enzyme	Pectolase – in liquid or powder form. The two enzymes break down the pectin in fruit and vegetables and are helpful in juice extraction and prevention of haze.
Sterilising agents	Campden tablets or sodium metabisulphite – to ensure protection from infection and oxidation.
Sugar	White household sugar is generally used, but brown sugar adds a deep, caramel flavour.
Tannin	Either as a powder or use a cup of tea, oak leaves, pear skins, black fruit.
Yeast	Specialist wine yeast, not baker's yeast – yeast ferments sugar as it reproduces in the presence of oxygen; when oxygen is cut off (e.g. when an airlock has been fitted) the yeast is forced to obtain its energy from the acid/sugar/nitrogen solution around it, converting sugar to alcohol and carbon dioxide (which bubbles out through the air lock).
Yeast Nutrients	Tablets or granules.

Method 1: Adding Yeast to Pulp

	Dessert Apple	Damson	Blackcurrant
Fruit	3 kg (6 lb), chopped	2 kg (4 lb), bruised	500 g (1 lb 2 oz)
Water	4 litres (6 pints)	4 litres (6 pints)	4 litres (6 pints)
Campden tablets	2	2	1½
Acid	Pectic enzyme	2 lemons - juice and rind	
Yeast	Wine yeast	Wine yeast	
Sugar	1.25 kg (2½ lb) white	1.5 kg (3 lb)	1.25 kg (2½ lb) white
Yeast Nutrients	Yes	Yes	Yes
Other Ingredients (optional)		15 g (½ oz) root ginger	Rohament P (if the blackcurrant juice is particularly viscous)

HOW TO LIVE ON LESS

1. Put 4 litres (6 pints) water into the polythene bin and dissolve the Campden tablets.
2. Remove stalks, wash fruit, remove stones, pith, etc. and then slice/dice larger fruit and drop into the water.
3. Add pectic enzyme.
4. Leave overnight.
5. Add yeast.
6. Cover the bin and keep at 15–20ºC (60–70ºF), squashing pulp at intervals to release the juice.
7. Leave for four days.
8. Dissolve yeast nutrients and sugar in the juice.
9. Strain off the pulp and pour the juice into a demijohn, and make up the volume with water to the shoulder of the vessel.
10. Insert a bung and airlock and maintain in the warm environment until bubbling through the airlock has stopped.
11. Siphon into sterilised bottles, label and leave to mature for at least six months.

Method 2: Adding Sugar to Pulp

	Strawberry*	**Rosehip**	**Honey**
Fruit	1.8 kg (4 lb), sliced Lemon rind	1 kg (2¼ lb), crushed (but not liquidised)	1.36 kg (3 lb) honey (dry) 1.8 kg (4 lb) (medium) 2.25 kg (5 lb) (sweet)
Water	4 litres (6 pints)	4 litres (6 pints)	Sufficient to make up to 4.5 litres (1 gallon)
Campden tablets	1	1	
Acid	Pectic enzyme	Pectic enzyme	10 g (½ oz) citric acid
Yeast	Wine yeast	Wine yeast	Sherry yeast
Sugar	1 kg (2¼ lb)	1.3 kg (3 lb) sugar	None
Yeast Nutrients	Yes	Yes	Two tablets
Other Ingredients (optional)	Cup of cold tea (tannin)		Cup of cold tea (tannin)

* Or use raspberries, gooseberries, blackberries, or a combination of any berries.

FOOD, DRINK AND A FEW BITS MORE

1. Place fruit or honey, tannin (if using) and sugar (if using) into the polythene bin.
2. Pour on boiling water, mashing down fruit; leave to cool.
3. Dissolve Campden tablets in a little hot water; add to bin with acid.
4. Leave overnight.
5. Add yeast, cover loosely and leave for one week, stirring daily, at 20–25°C (70–75°F).

Continue from Step 9, Method 1.

Method 3: Boiling Base to Extract Fluid

	Beetroot	**Broad Bean**	**Parsnip***
Vegetables	2.5 kg (5 lb)	1.5 kg	2 kg (4.5 lb)
Water	4 litres (6 pints)	4 litres (6 pints)	4 litres (6 pints)
Campden tablets	3	3	1
Acid	1 tsp pectic enzyme; 1 tsp tartaric acid		Pectic enzyme
Yeast	Wine yeast	Hock wine yeast	Madeira wine yeast
Sugar	1.25 kg (2½ lb)	1.25 kg (2½ lb)	1 kg (2¼ lb) Demerara
Yeast Nutrients	Yes	Yes	Yes
Other Ingredients (optional)	1 lemon, juice and rind	2 lemons, juice and rind	Cup of cold tea (tannin)

* Or use other individual root vegetables – carrots, potatoes, or combination of roots.

1. Wash the vegetables, cut into small cubes if necessary and put into a saucepan.
2. Add 4 litres (6 pints) water and grated lemon rind (if using); boil until tender then discard the pulp (or reuse in a soup).
3. Dissolve sugar, Campden tablets and nutrients in hot liquid; when cool add lemon juice (if using), tannin (if using) and pectic enzyme.
4. Leave overnight.
5. Add yeast, cover loosely and leave for one week, stirring daily, at 20–25°C (70–75°F).

Continue from Step 9, Method 1.

Method 4: Macerating

	Parsley	**Dandelion**	**Hawthorn**
Herb/Flower	375 g (13 oz) plus 250 g (9 oz) sultanas	2.5 litres (4 pints) (yellow parts only) plus 250 g (9 oz) sultanas	Flower
Water	5 litres (1 gallon)	5 litres (1 gallon)	5 litres (1 gallon) 5 litres (1 gallon)
Campden tablets	2	1	1
Acid	Citric acid	Citric acid	None
Yeast	Wine yeast	Wine yeast	Wine yeast
Sugar	1 kg (2¼ lb) white	1 kg (2¼ lb) white	1 kg (2¼ lb) white
Yeast Nutrients	Yes	Yes	Yes
Other Ingredients (optional)	Juice of 2 oranges	Fruit of 2 oranges (no pith)	Cup of cold tea (tannin) Juice and zest of 2 oranges (no pith)

1. Place herb/flower in the polythene bin with sultanas (if using) and orange juice/fruit/zest (if using).
2. Pour on 5 litres (1 gallon) boiling water; leave to cool.
3. Dissolve Campden tablets in a little hot water; add to bin with pectin enzyme.
4. Leave for 2–3 days.
5. Add sugar.
6. Add yeast and tannin (if using).

Continue from Step 9, Method 1.

Blending Different Wines

If, at the end of your production, you have a wine that is too dry, too sweet, lacking in tannin or needing more flavour/bouquet, never fear – try blending your wines. Each time you "open" your wine, all you need to remember is to add another Campden tablet and return the wine to a warm place to check for re-fermentation. Then siphon and bottle as usual.

FOOD, DRINK AND A FEW BITS MORE

Other Alcoholic Drinks

Quince Brandy

Ingredients
1 litre (1¾ pints) vodka or gin
175 g (6 oz) caster sugar
8 quinces
Two-litre large bottle with a sealable top (or a kilner jar), sterilised

Method
1. Peel the quince and grate the flesh coarsely – the peel and core can be thrown on the compost.

2. Put the grated quince and sugar into the bottle and pour over the vodka or gin.

3. Stir to dissolve as much sugar as you can.

4. Top up the bottle with water, seal, and place on the windowsill, or other sunny site.

5. Shake the jar every day for a couple of weeks to dissolve all the sugar.

6. Leave for a further two weeks until the liquid turns a rich, deep amber.

7. Strain through muslin, and bottle, seal and label.

Drink immediately, or keep it if you can!

Variations
This recipe also works well with cherries and damsons – no need to grate, just put them in the bottle with sugar. The fruit will need to fill about one-third of the bottle.

Add cinnamon sticks and a large pinch of whole cloves.

Sloe Gin

1. Remove stalks from 250 g (9 oz) sloes, and wash and prick at both ends.

2. Place in a large kilner jar with 125 g (4½ oz) sugar.

3. Top up the jar with 400 ml (14 fl oz) gin; seal and shake vigorously.

4. Shake the jar twice a day for 3–4 weeks.

5. Leave to mature for at least one year.

6. Strain through muslin, and bottle, seal and label.

Strawberry Margarita

1. Chill two cocktail glasses.

2. Liquidise a handful of strawberries (for two people) with 1 tbsp lime juice.

3. Add 90 ml (3 fl oz) Tequila and 30 ml (1 fl oz) Cointreau and whiz until combined.

4. Add crushed ice, or throw in some cubes and whiz briefly.

5. Dip the rims of the cocktail glasses in lime juice and then into sugar to provide a frosted effect.

6. Pour the Margarita into the glasses and serve.

Non-Alcoholic Drinks

Reality Check: ϒ ☺ ££-

Fruit and Vegetable Juices

Freshly made fruit and vegetable juices are incredibly refreshing, tasty and invigorating. If you have never tasted freshly squeezed carrot juice, either "naked" or spiked with beetroot or ginger, then you are missing a real treat! It is so sweet and luscious. You'd never think such an innocuous root vegetable could produce such a smooth and tasty drink.

FOOD, DRINK AND A FEW BITS MORE

Fresh juices are packed with all the goodness and health benefits of raw food, delivered in an easy-to-drink and easy-to-digest form, free from added sugar, caffeine, salt and fat. If you have grown the fruit and vegetables yourself, your ingredients will have cost you next to nothing, and you will know that the raw ingredients are 100% organic.

You will need to purchase a juicing machine – I prefer the centrifugal variety – which will cost you anything from £35 to £150 depending on what size motor you go for and the additional facilities offered. After that, it's really down to your imagination what combinations of fruit and/or vegetables you use. Some vegetable juices like beetroot can taste incredibly "earthy", which you may or may not like, but anyway tend to be overpowering on their own; others like cabbage come through with a rawness that is frankly not palatable, but mixed together – with some apple, celery, maybe a hint lemon grass – are quite delicious as well as nutritious. You can develop a range of juice mixes to suit your taste and what you have available. Whatever you do, don't add sugar! If you need the juice to be sweeter, add some additional fruit.

Smoothies
If you are keeping an eye on your weight, you can't beat a thick fruit smoothie for breakfast. It will not only make your stomach feel satisfied that it's been given something to start the day, but you'll also be taking in a rich cocktail of essential vitamins and minerals. I make my smoothies so thick that I use a spoon to eat them and I like to float fresh berries on the top and eat them gradually as the smoothie descends down the glass. I also prefer to use fresh fruit for my smoothies, but my niece Emma and her boyfriend Louis keep a stash of frozen berries that they whiz up in the morning and drink through a straw.

You will need a blender, or a dedicated smoothie maker, which will cost you from £9 to £35. After that, it's down to you – just throw in your preferred fruit and whiz together. You can use single fruit, e.g. a mango or two to produce a tasty smoothie, or try different combinations. Bananas and avocado help to make a smoothie rich and creamy; oranges and pineapple make it loose and juicy. If you like your smoothie to be drinkable rather than thick and spoonable, then just add fruit (or vegetable) juice or water to the fruit. I am personally not a fan of adding milk or yoghurt to a smoothie – why contaminate with dairy produce when you can drink pure fruit? But everyone's different and you might like to give it a try.

HOW TO LIVE ON LESS

Dandelion Coffee

My dad always drank "Camp" coffee – I think it probably reminded him of something he drank during the war – and as kids it's what we knew as coffee before we got older and wiser and discovered that "real" coffee actually came in instant-powder form.

Dandelion is in fact a close cousin to chicory, which is the predominant herb in Camp coffee, and makes a splendid substitute.

As you will be using the roots of the dandelion, ensure your source can be dug up legally – either from your own garden or with the permission of the landowner.

Method
1. Dig up the long dandelion tap roots.
2. Cut off the leaves (you can use the nice young ones in a salad and fry the rest in bacon fat).
3. Clean the roots thoroughly, ensuring there is no trace of soil.
4. Slice the roots into chunks – you eventually need to be able to get them into a grinder.
5. Dry the roots over a period of about two weeks, turning every day.
6. Roast the dried root in a low oven at 160°C (325°F, gas 3) for about 15–20 minutes until dark brown inside.
6a. Steps 5 and 6 can be combined by roasting undried in a medium oven at 200°C with the door ajar to allow moisture to escape. This method roasts and dries at the same time.
7. Grind in a coffee grinder.

Use
Allow 2 tsp per root per person: put into a coffee pot or a tisane jug.
Pour over boiling water and steep for 3–5 minutes.
Use a tea strainer to filter out any pieces.
Drink as you would normal coffee, on its own, with milk or with cream, and/or sweetened with honey.

FOOD, DRINK AND A FEW BITS MORE

Livestock

Everyone I have ever met that keeps livestock either commercially (i.e. a farmer) or as part of their self-sufficient lifestyle talks of their animals fondly, as a rewarding part of their life, yet without the emotion or sentimentality generally associated with keeping household pets. None more so than my girlfriend Gill's husband, Ahmet, who was raised on a farm in Cyprus. Both of his parents' families had kept livestock all their lives – predominantly sheep and goats – and his grandfather had been a shepherd. Ahmet talked to me of the natural cycle of life – how with good animal husbandry and a lot of TLC the animals were raised with dignity and care for the milk, butter and cheese they produced, and then either sold or slaughtered to provide income and meat for the table. His mindset is clearly one of giving an animal a decent life in preparation for its eventual end, which was ultimately a contribution to the family's income, there being no other form of work in the area they lived.

These days in the UK, Ahmet and Gill don't keep any livestock because they feel their lifestyle is not geared up to the commitment needed to raise animals – they like their holidays, and want to spend quality time with their children and grandchildren, Gill spends her mornings (with me) in the gym and Ahmet loves his golf. While some of these activities can be fitted in around livestock, it really isn't practical to spend several weeks away and expect the neighbour to look after your pigs! Chickens, maybe, could be looked after while you're away if you don't have a large flock, but few people are capable (even if willing) to tend to bees, unless they are confident they know what they are doing.

Your own mindset, therefore, is going to dictate whether you include livestock in your living-on-less strategy, and what form of livestock that might be. The rewards for rearing animals are numerous – as well as knowing you are providing a good life for working animals, you will get to enjoy their different personalities as they grow from infancy to maturity, and along the way you receive in return the products of their life, whether that be eggs, milk, cheese, honey or meat. If you are sensitive to killing, or to sending your animals away for slaughter, or even to eating the meat of the livestock you have raised, then perhaps raising livestock for meat production is not for you.

In this section I'm going to describe how six people I have met raise livestock as part of their self-sufficient lifestyle, highlighting the joys and the drawbacks along the way. I've limited my coverage to bees, chickens and pigs, as they seem to provide three different levels of animal husbandry and may give you an insight into what is required. However, you could make other choices such as geese, ducks, goats, sheep, cows or even llamas and alpacas. Whichever you choose, don't underestimate the commitment you need to make, but also anticipate the joy that raising animals will bring and the major contribution they will make to your living-on-less lifestyle.

Beekeeping

Reality Check: ♈ ♈ ☺☺ ££- £+ ♥

Why Keep Bees?
I've known Piers for many years as a colleague at work and he has enjoyed following a passion for beekeeping learned as a child from his grandparents. While researching for this book, I was also privileged to meet Marian and Pete Bracey. Marian keeps chickens – more about her later in this Livestock section – and her husband Pete keeps bees: he took up beekeeping as one of his retirement projects.

Bees are an important element of organic gardening, as they pollinate flowers in their search for nectar in your border, on the vegetable patch and in the herb garden. When Piers' grandparents first decided to keep bees, they sited their hives close to the mature orchard that was part of their garden. That season, the yield of fruit doubled and continued at a high level for their remaining beekeeping years – testimony to the fact that bees are prodigious pollinators. And last year Pete was asked by a neighbouring farmer who had planted a field of borage to bring his bees over "on loan" to pollinate the flowers.

> ① Did you know...? Albert Einstein has been credited with the quotation, "If the bee disappeared off the surface of the globe, then man would only have four years of life left." Whether he actually said it or not is open to debate, but what it does highlight is just how important bees are to pollination...if they weren't around to do this important job, maybe we wouldn't be around for much longer either!

As well as providing this useful pollinating service, bees also produce a supply of honey and beeswax – about 27 kg (60 lb) honey per hive – certainly more than enough honey than you'll ever get through yourself,

FOOD, DRINK AND A FEW BITS MORE

leaving plenty of surplus for gifts, sale or barter. Organic, single-source honey from the supermarket costs 73.2p per 100 g (£3.29 per 450 g); a home-produced honey generally sells at around £3 per 450 g.

The urban bee, in fact, may be better off in his environment than his country cousin. Cities and towns tend to be warmer, providing a longer foraging season. The wide variety of domestic flower borders as well as council-planted gardens, parks and roundabouts provide a source of nectar close to the hive, meaning the bees don't have to use up too much energy foraging.

With care and with the right clothing and equipment, beekeeping is both safe and enjoyable. Bees have a strong social network within the hive, depending on each other for survival, and are fascinating to watch. Also, unlike the aggressive wasp, it's not in a bee's nature to sting, unless truly provoked. After all, a bee literally has to lay down its life in order to sting. Protective clothing generally prevents bee stings, but occasionally one occurs and the normal reactions include pain and swelling at the sting site. If you do get stung, remember that the sting continues to pump out venom for about two minutes, so it's well worth pulling out the sting quickly if you can. However, if you know that you, or the people around you, have an allergic reaction to bee or wasp stings, then beekeeping may not be for you.

Getting Started
Spring is the time when beekeeping associations are dividing up their hives and looking to sell a nucleus of bees to a newcomer. A nucleus will have a laying queen, several pounds of bees, drawn comb in which the queen is already laying eggs, and some honey and pollen stores.

Before you buy, however, you do need to ensure you have the right clothing and equipment, and a suitable site for your hive. The novice should start with either one or two hives. You can add more once you have got some experience with the annual beekeeping cycle – but be aware that once you keep hives, new swarms of bees do tend to find you, looking for a new home. Pete tells me it's because they can smell the honey and wax, and know they're going to be well looked after.

It is possible to buy second-hand hives and equipment, but you really need to know what you are doing. As a novice you may fall into some of the pitfalls of buying second hand and completely spoil your first experiences of beekeeping. It may be better in the long run to buy new.

HOW TO LIVE ON LESS

Key beekeeping equipment comprises:

- Protective clothing
- Beehive with tools and accessories
- Bees
- Bee health products and remedies
- Extracting, filtering and bottling equipment
- Honey jars and labels
- Record book and beekeeping books
- Insurance

Time to Break Even

To calculate the Time to Break Even, just one hive and the expected maximum yield of 27 kg (60 lb) have been assumed.

Cost of beekeeping equipment	£300 (estimated)
Honey produced	27 kg (60 lb)
Honey for own use	2 kg (5 lb) = 2,000 g
Price of supermarket single-source organic honey	73.2p per 100 g
Saving on purchased organic honey	Honey for own use times price from supermarket 2,000 g / 100 g x 73.2p = 1,464p = £14.64
Surplus honey	25 kg (55 lb)
Price of home-produced honey	£3 per 450 g (1 lb) jar
Number of 450 g (1 lb) jars	25 kg / 450 g = 55
Income from surplus honey	Number of jars times price of 55 x 3 = £165
Combined savings and income	Saving plus income £14.64 + £165 = £179.64
Time to Break Even months	£300 / £179.64 = 1 year 8

The Hive and its Bees

Drone — The only males in the colony – typically around 300 per hive. They spend their lives down the pub, generally boasting of how they will perform when they eventually mate with the queen, little knowing that when they do she will rip out their genitalia for the all-important sperm sack and then leave them to die a horrible death. Those that remain alive at the end of the year will be driven out by the worker bees to die in the cold.

FOOD, DRINK AND A FEW BITS MORE

Foundation	A rectangle of wax separated into tiny hexagons on which the bees build (draw) and form the comb into which honey is deposited and eggs are laid; the foundation sits inside a frame.
Frame	A slim wooden frame which encloses a foundation and sits inside the super.
Super	Wooden box, filled with 11 frames, which sits inside the hive to collect honey or act as a brood chamber.
Swarming	Queen leaves the hive, potentially taking more than half the colony with her.
Queen bee	A mature female. She lays thousands of eggs during her lifetime and has the longest lifespan in the colony, living for up to five years. The queen is a larger bee than the workers.
Queen cup	Empty cells built in preparation for queen larvae.
Queen excluder	Frame or partition which prevents the queen from entering and laying her eggs in the honey store.
Varroa mite	These carry a virus which affects bees.
Varroa strips	Strips containing chemicals that are slowly released into the hive that kill the Varroa mite.
Worker bees	Sexually underdeveloped females that do all the chores – collect food and water, build wax comb, do the housework, keep the temperature nice and cosy, and chase off intruders. They lay eggs, but because they are not mated the eggs only develop into drones. Can be up to 60,000 worker bees per colony.

Choosing a Site for Your Hive

The area where you put your beehives need not be very large, but it does need to be on flat ground. The hives should be open to the Southeast so that they are oriented towards the morning sun and with a clear flight path out, in a location that does not get many passers-by – out of sight, out of mind! Remember: you may not be afraid of bees, but other people are – and if they happen to get stung (even if it's by a wasp), it's always going to be one of "your" bees that's the culprit! The bottom of the garden is an ideal location, or even on a sheltered, flat roof like a garage. Either way, try to arrange for the flight path to start in an upwards direction – over a fence, hedge or shrub border – as this will help keep bees away from people: once bees are up in the air, they disperse every which way. Also, you will need an element of shade. Not only do the bees need to keep cool

HOW TO LIVE ON LESS

when the weather turns really hot, but you've also got to work there, in a full body suit! Once you've chosen your site, find something to raise the height of your hive to the height that you want to work at, otherwise you will be bending over all the time.

How Bees Make Honey and Wax
Once a bee is mature, around three weeks, it is ready to collect nectar and will continue to do this for the rest of its life, a further five weeks. Bees are known to fly up to two miles or more to find nectar, but if nectar sources are close to the hive less time is spent flying and foraging, so more trips can be made per day. The type of honey produced depends on what flowers and foliage exist in your area. Unless you can control foraging to a single-source of nectar then you are likely to end up with a blended honey.

The bee filters nectar through its mouth, along the gut and into the honey sac that has a capacity of 40 to 70 mg. Collecting nectar effectively doubles the bee's body weight. On returning to the hive, the nectar is delivered to the house bees and the foraging bee returns to the garden. As the bees pass the liquid honey from worker to worker and into the cells of the comb, the bees dry the honey until the sugar content increases to around 80% – at which stage, once the cells are full, they cap them with wax for storage.

The Annual Beekeeping Cycle
There is a very clear cycle to the beekeeping year:

Oct-Jan
Bees don't hibernate, but they are not particularly active during the winter months. You will need to provide a supply of feed in the form of sugar syrup and keep a check that the entrance is clear of any blockages – particularly dead bees – and secure from mice. Also provide some water nearby for the bees to drink. Pete puts water in a plant saucer filled with stones so that the bees can land on a stone and take a drink, otherwise they may drown if it's too deep. Drones will be expelled from the hive during the winter, having completed their life's short but sweet assignment, and will be left to die.

Feb-Mar
The queen bee starts to lay eggs in February. Gently heft (lift) the hive to check food weight and if it is light continue to fill the bees' feeder with sugar syrup. As the weather warms up, the colony will grow quickly and

FOOD, DRINK AND A FEW BITS MORE

food consumption will increase considerably. Although it's spring, there still isn't enough pollen around for bees to forage, so it's down to you to keep the feeder topped up.

April-May
Bees will fly out on warm days to gather what nectar and pollen they can from the spring blossoms, and the brood starts to increase. Fit a queen excluder to stop the queen getting to the honey store. Add new supers as necessary to make space for the growing colony. If you are lucky enough, you might see a "Bee Dance": scout bees fly off in search of nectar then return to the hive and "dance" to convey to the worker bees the precise location, coordinates, bearing, distance – literally, "X" marks the spot – of the nectar they have found. You'll see a lot of wing-flapping, circling, figure-of-eight, tail-waggling, etc.

June-Aug
Summer is a busy time in the beekeeping calendar – pollen and nectar are in abundance, and the beekeeper's skill is needed to prevent swarming. Check your hive regularly, adding and removing supers, looking all the time for signs of disease. Queen cups should be destroyed by squashing them with a hive tool. Frames of capped honey or even complete supers can be removed – make sure you have empty frames or supers to replace those taken – and by early August you should pretty much have your full harvest. Reduce the size of the entrance to keep out hive "robbers" – wasps are the most likely predators. The guard bees can patrol a smaller entrance quite easily.

Aug-Sep
Once you've removed the honey store and effectively taken away the bees' winter food supply, add sugar syrup to their feeder so that the bees have a source of energy. Each colony will need around 2.25 kg (5 lb) sugar made into syrup to make it through the winter months. Insert Varroa strips to guard against the Varroa mite. Now that you have completed your harvest, you will need to extract the honey and melt down the wax.

Harvesting Honey and Wax
A single, deep frame full of honey will weigh around 2.7 kg (6 lb); an established colony can produce up to 27 kg (60 lb) honey from one hive. That means you've got to be prepared to harvest, extract, sieve, sterilise, bottle and label that quantity of produce. It's no mean feat! Honey can be removed from a hive almost any time provided that it is fully capped over with wax, so you could start the bottling process during the summer. Pete harvests some of his honey early in the year because his bees forage on oil

seed rape, which flowers early in the season and produces a honey that crystallises quickly. He then has time to catch the next round of pollen – maybe from his borage-growing farmer friend – to produce a different style of honey. If your frames are not fully capped, the unripe honey will spoil by absorbing moisture. Once the moisture content exceeds 18.6%, honey will tend to ferment, turning the sugars of the honey into alcohol and spoiling your end product with a sour taste.

Extracting Honey
First, you need to take off the wax capping with a hot knife. Like attempting to cut the peel from an apple in one long, curly strip, it takes a bit of skill to get your wax capping off in one piece; but it's well worth it if you want to make rolled beeswax candles – see the instructions at the end of the Beekeeping section.

Both Piers and Pete have used plastic, hand-cranked centrifuges that were loaned from their respective beekeeping societies to extract their honey. Pete has since invested in a stainless steel electric version – he has seven hives and 190 kg (420 lb) honey to deal with, so it was a wise investment, though strangely he doesn't even like the taste of honey! Once extracted, the honey needs to be sieved twice – once to remove the obvious, coarse floating bits, and a second time through muslin and a fine sieve to make sure it's completely clear. It can then be decanted into clean, sterilised jars, sealed and labelled.

If you have the time, patience and a completely squeaky-clean environment, you can also process the comb, and separate the honey from the wax, using the following self-sufficient method. This method is particularly useful for a beginner because the hive may not generate the target amount of honey in its first year – particularly if you start mid-season – and there's no additional outlay on specialist equipment.

In a clean environment:

1. Place a filter, e.g. muslin or cheesecloth, over a large food-grade storage container.
2. Scrape the honey from the foundation – the wax comb and honey come off easily using the hive tool – into the filter cloth.
3. Allow the honey to filter through the cloth into the container; the wax will remain in the cloth. Note that this step can take as long as 24 hours to complete.

FOOD, DRINK AND A FEW BITS MORE

4. Squeeze the wax until as much of the honey as possible is out.
5. Mix the remaining wax with water. This will clean the wax ready for use, and the resultant honey-water can be used for feeding the bees over winter.
6. Decant the honey into clean, sterilised jars, label and seal.

Pure honey will last a long time, though it does darken with age. Avoid fermentation and granulation (when a sugar-like substance is produced). Granulated honey can be returned to its liquid state by gently heating it in a bain-marie (water bath) at 95–120°F.

Using Honey

> ⓘ Did you know...? Some hay fever sufferers find it beneficial to eat honey – the small quantity of pollen ingested acts as a natural immunization.

Honey is a completely natural product, a good preservative with all toxins taken out by bees. It is great just spread on bread or mixed with hot milk and whisky as a night-time sleeping aid, particularly if you have a cold. Or why not try making mead?

Wax

No-melt Rolled Beeswax Candles
If you've been successful in cutting off your wax capping into one, neat rectangle, you can quickly create two pretty rolled candles.

Method
1. Purchase a wick suitable for the finished diameter and cut it 2.5 cm (1") longer than the height of the short side of the beeswax rectangle.

2. Cut the beeswax rectangle in half from corner to corner, resulting in two triangles.

3. Place the wick along the side of the triangle that used to be short side of the beeswax rectangle.

4. Drizzle a little molten beeswax along the longest side of the triangle (the hypotenuse – the edge that was cut corner-to-corner): this will help to make the edge stick.

5. Fold the wax over the wick and roll up the whole triangle evenly, making sure the base of the candle is level (if necessary you can cut it straight afterwards with a hot knife). As you roll, press the edge gently against the rest of the candle to make sure it remains in one piece.

6. Trim the wick to 5 mm ($1/4$") and dip the end into molten beeswax to prime it.

Melting Wax
(Caution: wax is very flammable: never melt over a naked flame. Always work in a well-ventilated place.)

1. Use a stainless steel pot (not iron because it will discolour the wax) and pour water into it about halfway up.
2. Place the wax into the pot and set over a controllable source of heat: Note: Wax melts at 63°C (148°F): do not allow the wax and water to boil.
3. Once the wax melts it will float to the surface.
4. Take the pot off the heat and allow to cool overnight.
5. The next day the wax will be a sold block, separated from the water.
6. On the bottom of the block will be a dark material, which is not wax but "slum gum". A wax press would get rid of this under pressure, but is not cost-effective for a small amount of wax. Scrape off the slum gum from the bottom of the wax block.

Wax will keep indefinitely. If your harvest is too small to use, keep it and add to it next year. Beekeeping societies generally purchase wax from their members – either at a cost of around £2 per 450 g (1 lb) wax, or in exchange for new foundations. From a purchaser's perspective, beeswax is a luxury item – so if you intend to sell or barter it, bear that in mind.

Furniture Polish
Ingredients
110 g (4 oz) clean, strained beeswax
15 g ($1/2$ oz) grated olive oil-based soap*
426 ml ($3/4$ pint) pure turpentine
$1/2$ tsp raw linseed oil
150 ml ($1/4$ pint) strong infusion of sweet marjoram**
90 g (3 oz) tins (wide-topped containers) for storing polish
* More or less soap will make the wax harder or softer respectively.
** Lemon balm, lemon verbena, rosemary or lavender flowers can replace sweet marjoram.

FOOD, DRINK AND A FEW BITS MORE

Method
- Melt wax and soap together in a plastic container (e.g. former milk or detergent bottle, with a handle) in a bain-marie. Make sure the grated soap is fully melted before continuing.
- Strain the wax through a piece of cotton (e.g. an old T-shirt).
- Measure the turpentine and linseed out and warm them together in another plastic container in the bain-marie.
- Add the herbal tea to the turpentine and linseed mix.
- Mix the fluids with the wax, pour into the containers, and label.

To use, apply a thin layer to wooden surfaces with a fine cloth, allow to set for one minute and then buff with a duster or fine cloth.

Keeping Chickens

Reality Check: ⍦ ① ££- £+

What would be your objective for keeping chickens? Producing a regular supply of fresh eggs, providing meat for the table, breeding, or a combination of all three? The reason I ask is that you will purchase different breeds of hen depending on what your objective is, and the lifecycle and approach for the three results is completely different. Whatever you decide to raise, always buy more than one chicken. Single hens will get lonely and may not lay eggs or fatten up as they should. They are sociable animals and appreciate company of their own kind.

Dedicated egg layers may be kept for up to five years, though two years is their best laying period and will produce around 200 delicious eggs per year (hybrid breeds, the best egg layers, may well produce more). They could eventually be cooked for the pot. Pure breeds rather than hybrids are better for this; however, their meat tends to be a bit tough, so you need to think slow-cooked casseroles like "coq au vin" (which, as the name suggests, is traditionally made from the cockerel – not the most tender of meats).

Dedicated meat producers, on the other hand, will be raised until they are around 14–18 weeks before they are despatched.

In between the two are dual-purpose birds that get fattened up more than dedicated egg-layers but still lay eggs, so you sort of get the best of both worlds, but these birds do not produce nearly as many eggs, and are not quite as plump for meat.

HOW TO LIVE ON LESS

Deciding the Size of Your Flock
As I mentioned above, always have at least two hens. Clearly you will also need a cockerel if you want to breed hens, but otherwise a male isn't required.

We have already met Marian Bracey in the section on Beekeeping, and I was introduced to Munira Grainger, sister of my long-term friend Mohsin, to hear her talk passionately about hens and allotments. Both Marian and Munira keep chickens for eggs but have chosen significantly different flock sizes. Coincidentally, both have chosen to keep Light Sussex-Rhode Island hybrids, as experience has shown them to be the best egg layers.

Small Scale
Munira has kept hens on and off for many years, and also a pair of ducks before the fox got the better of them. When she bought the most recent two hens – purchased "at point of lay" for about £12 each – she also bought an "eglu" from an Internet Auction Site to house them in.

If you've never seen an eglu, then I urge you to visit the site at www.omlet.co.uk. It's made by a company called Omlet (I kid you not) and is quite the latest thing in "urban chic" (I'm sorry, that's a really fowl joke!). Munira's eglu is green, but if buying from new you can select whatever colour takes your fancy. The eglu comes with a run of 2 m, but Munira and her husband extended this to 3 m to give the hens a bit more space. It's easy to clean, fox-proof and lightweight to move around, so they tend to move the location of the run each week to give the hens nice fresh grass to eat, and a chance for their lawn to recover. Omlet also provide a wealth of advice, and can provide specialist products (e.g. feed, worming powder) if needed.

In the past, Munira just let her hens have the full run of their 60 ft garden, but they are such voracious grass eaters (and, incidentally, pond weed, which can be helpful) that the hens quickly devastated the entire lawn. Instead they are fed lettuces and carrot tops which Munira brings back from her allotment every afternoon, plus any scraps of rice, pasta and potatoes that she has left over from feeding the family. Actually, not just scraps – I happen to know that she cooks extra simply to give it to the hens. This is in addition to their regular diet of fresh grain, grit, layers' pellets and whatever they can forage for in the garden.

FOOD, DRINK AND A FEW BITS MORE

Generally speaking, both hens lay an egg each per day, thus producing a dozen eggs or so between them in a week, although the quantity gets reduced over the winter months. That's definitely sufficient to provide Munira's family with enough eggs for breakfasts, lunches or baking, but typically no surplus for sale, though Munira does provide gift packages of fruit, vegetables and eggs to friends and family on their birthdays.

A typical chicken day at Munira's house starts in the morning when her husband opens the door to the eglu before he goes to work. If the sun's not up, the hens simply wait indoors until it's daylight before they venture out. If it's a miserable day, they may not even bother to leave the coop – but it's their choice. Grain and water are put out for them to eat and drink and they spend their day scratching the grass. During the early morning they lay their eggs, announcing each arrival by putting their heads in the air and singing a chorus or two. In the afternoon, armed with green goodies from the allotment, Munira provides a leafy treat and collects the eggs. In the evening, once the hens have naturally returned into the eglu, the chicken coop door is closed for the night.

Time to Break Even *Hens with Infrastructure (Eglu)*

Cost to start Eglu (new) Two hens at point of lay Annual feed for two hens	£400 (estimated)
Quantity of eggs produced per year	Two hens times 200 each 2 x 200 = 400 = 33.33 dozen
Price of organic eggs per dozen	£3.65
Annual saving on purchase of eggs	Quantity of eggs times price of eggs 33.33 x £3.65 = £121.65
Time to Break Even	Cost to start divided by annual saving £400 / £121.65 = 3 years 3 months

After this initial investment and break-even period, you would almost certainly be purchasing new hens, but not investing in any further infrastructure. The Time to Break Even on this second and future phase of hens is much quicker and similar to purchasing hens without infrastructure (e.g. using existing outbuildings).

Hens without Infrastructure

Cost to continue Two hens at point of lay (£12 each = £24) Annual feed for two hens (£50 estimated)	£24 + £50 = £74 (estimated)
Quantity of eggs produced per year	Two hens times 200 each 2 x 200 = 400 = 33.33 dozen
Price of organic eggs per dozen	£3.65
Annual saving on purchase of eggs	Quantity of eggs times price of eggs 33.33 x £3.65 = £121.65
Time to Break Even	Cost to continue divided by annual saving £74 / £121.65 = 7 months

Larger Scale

Marian's chicken-keeping is on a much larger scale – she currently has 40 hens – and they have a slightly different lifestyle to Munira's, occupying a couple of barns and sharing the run of the garden with a couple of geese (so much better than guard dogs!) and her husband's seven hives of bees. Like Munira, Marian keeps mainly Rhode Island-Light Sussex cross, but she also has Silkie, Plymouth Rock and Sussex breeds.

With the larger number of hens around her, Marian is able to see a variety of different personalities among the population and witness some incredibly tribal temperaments. She has one hen that insists on laying her eggs over the road close to a neighbour's house. The hen has been kept at home in detention several times – the usual way to (re-)train a hen where she belongs – but still she hops back across the road. Also, adding new stock to an existing flock can cause enormous problems. We've all heard the expression "hen-pecked" – well, Marian sees this with regularity when new hens are introduced, even when quarantined for a short period while the existing flock get used to them. The existing hens don't like the newcomers (in fact her flock also took umbrage at a whole new breed of hen) and so peck at the feathers around the vent, eventually pecking deeper for more internal damage that we won't go into here. But this does give a very clear warning: if you are going to keep chickens, particularly in small number, do purchase them all at the same time, as otherwise you'll find it's the other hens and not just foxes that are the predators.

FOOD, DRINK AND A FEW BITS MORE

Time to Break Even

Given the quantity of hens being reared, Marian has plenty of surplus eggs for sale, gift or barter. She has also reused existing outbuildings, and so has not had to invest in a specialist chicken coop; but she has made a significant investment in purchasing 400 hens, the associated feed, and egg boxes with which to sell produce.

Cost to start 400 hens at point of lay (£10* each = £4,000) Annual feed for 400 hens, plus egg boxes, worming powder and other incidentals (£10,000 estimated)	£4,000 + £10,000 = £14,000 (estimated)
Quantity of eggs produced per year 400 hens times 200 each	400 x 200 = 80,000 = 6,666.66 dozen
Quantity of eggs for personal use	51.66 dozen (i.e. roughly a dozen per week)
Annual saving on purchase of eggs	Quantity of eggs times price of eggs 51.66 x £3.65 = £188.56
Quantity of eggs for sale	6,615 dozen
Price of organic home- produced eggs per dozen	£3.20
Revenue from sale of eggs	Quantity of eggs times price of eggs 6,615 x £3.20 = £21,168
Total income and saving	Annual saving plus revenue £188.56 + £21,168 = £21,356.56
Time to Break Even	Cost to start divided by total income and saving £14,000 / £21,356.56 = 8 months

* I have assumed a discount on Marian's hens over Munira's as she is buying a large quantity. You could also spend significantly less if you purchase newborn chicks and rear them yourself rather than hens at point of lay.

Good Healthy Chickens

When you go to buy your hens, and throughout their lifetime, look out for healthy good looks:

- dry nostrils and bright, beady eyes
- red comb
- glossy feathers, all present and plumped up
- good weight and musculature, plump and firm with a fleshy breastbone

- clean vent (rear end); feathers with no smell
- alert and active
- no visible fleas or lice close to the body

Obviously, with recent outbreaks of avian flu in the UK, it would make sense to keep an eye on the news for any alerts, and take advice from Defra (the Department for Environment, Food and Rural Affairs): www.defra.gov.uk.

Natural Pest Control (Chickens)

Flies: Dried pyrethrum (Tanacetum cinerariifolium) strewn in the chicken coop will deter flies.

Fox: Human hair – stuffed into the cut-off lower leg of a pair of tights and tied to the fence of your chicken run. It seems Mr Fox doesn't like the smell of humans any more than we like the smell of him, and our hair is a particularly rich source of the oils that give us our distinctive scent.

Lice: Hang a large bunch of dried wormwood (Artemisia absinthum) inside the coop and add some dried leaves to the chickens' bedding straw.

Mice: Tansy (Tanacetum vulgare) should keep the mice away.

Using Produce from Chickens

Manure
This is probably not the reason you keep hens in the first place, but nevertheless it is a nitrogen-rich by-product that should always be added to the compost heap.

Eggs
Until you've eaten a perfect, fresh-laid egg, you won't appreciate just how tasty it is. Whether fried, boiled, scrambled or made into an omelette, home-produced eggs are a rich, deep yellow and absolutely delicious. Here are some of my favourite egg recipes that use produce from the kitchen garden.

Tortilla Española
This is a tasty, versatile dish that can either be served warm as a main course for two people, as one of a selection of tapas, or cold, cut into squares, as part of a finger buffet.

FOOD, DRINK AND A FEW BITS MORE

Ingredients
6 eggs
200 ml (7 fl oz) light olive oil (not virgin or extra-virgin)
1 small potato, peeled and diced
1 small onion, finely chopped
4 cloves garlic (reduce the quantity if you prefer), finely chopped
Large pinch coarse salt

Method
1. Sweat the onions and the garlic gently in the oil in a large, heavy frying pan, but do not allow the vegetables to brown.

2. Add the potatoes in one layer with the coarse salt and cook very slowly, partially covered, until the potatoes are tender; stir occasionally so that the potatoes remain as individual dice and do not stick together.

3. Drain the vegetables through a sieve, reserving 3 tbsp of the oil for cooking the tortilla. (Any remaining oil can be kept and reused for another recipe.)

4. Beat the eggs with 1 tbsp water until they are slightly foamy.

5. Add the vegetables to the eggs and stir so that they become fully coated in egg. Leave to stand for at least 15 minutes so that the potatoes absorb some of the egg.

6. Heat 2 tbsp of the reserved oil in the same frying pan until it reaches smoking point. Swish the oil over the whole of the base pan, making sure it goes up the sides as well.

7. Pour in the egg-and-potato mixture and cook over a medium heat until the eggs have browned underneath.

8. Place a plate over the frying pan, and turn the whole thing over so that the omelette falls out onto the plate.

9. Add the remaining 1 tbsp oil to the frying pan, wait until it is hot, then slide the omelette back into the pan, uncooked-side-down, to finish cooking.

10. Transfer to a serving platter and leave to stand for 5–10 minutes before cutting and serving warm, or leave to cool completely for a buffet.

Île Flottante

I love this French dessert. If you don't recognise the name (which translates as Floating Island), it's meringue floating on a sea of cooled vanilla custard. Divine!

Ingredients
Meringue:
8 egg whites
pinch of salt
250 g (9 oz) sugar
Small knob butter (for greasing)
25 g (1 oz) toasted almonds

Custard:
8 egg yolks
1 litre (1¾ pints) milk
1 vanilla pod
250 g (9 oz) caster sugar

Method
1. Whisk the egg whites with a pinch of salt and half the sugar until it forms soft peaks.

2. Gradually incorporate the rest of the sugar.

3. Butter an ovenproof dish (or four individual dishes) and sprinkle with caster sugar; place the meringue into the dish and place the whole into a bain-marie.

4. Cook for 20 minutes at 150°C (300°F, gas mark 2) or until it no longer sticks to your fingers when lightly touched.

5. Remove from the oven and allow to cool, then turn out into a serving bowl, or individual bowls.

6. Bring the milk to the boil with the split vanilla pod and half the caster sugar, then take off the heat and leave to infuse for 5–10 minutes.

7. Beat the egg yolks and the remaining caster sugar together until pale and creamy.

FOOD, DRINK AND A FEW BITS MORE

8. Remove the vanilla pod, then pour the milk in a thin stream over the eggs, whisking constantly.

9. Return the mixture to the saucepan and heat gently, stirring all the time to avoid it getting lumpy until it reaches simmering point. At this point it should lightly coat the back of a wooden spoon.

10. Strain and leave to cool.

11. Pour the custard around the island and sprinkle toasted almonds over the top.

Meat

Pot Roast Chicken with Juniper Berries

Ingredients
2 tbsp light olive oil
2 cloves garlic, crushed
1 large onion, half finely chopped, half in chunks
2 tsp juniper berries, crushed
Freshly milled black pepper
1 home-raised chicken – make sure it fits into your casserole
1 carrot, sliced
1 leek, sliced
2 sticks celery, sliced
2 bay or myrtle leaves
450 ml (¾ pint) chicken stock

Method
1. Make a marinade with 1 tbsp oil, garlic, finely chopped onion, juniper and pepper; rub the outside of the chicken with the marinade then put any remaining marinade into the cavity. Cover and leave to absorb the flavours for about an hour.

2. Heat the remaining oil and brown the chicken all over; remove.

3. Add the chunked onion, carrot, leek and celery and cook very gently until the onion is translucent.

4. Return the chicken to the casserole and add the stock and bay or myrtle leaves.

5. Cover and cook on the hob over a medium heat or in the oven at 180°C (350°F, gas mark 4) for about an hour. Test whether the chicken is cooked by piercing the thick part of a leg with a skewer – the juices should run clear. Ensure all the juices from inside the chicken are added to the casserole.

6. If the juices of the casserole seem a little thin, remove the vegetables with a slotted spoon and keep warm while you reduce the gravy by rapid boiling.

7. Carve the chicken in serving pieces and serve with the vegetables and gravy.

Variation
A small glass of gin added towards the end of cooking will enhance the juniper flavour.

Pigs

For many people the first foray into raising livestock is often to keep chickens, but soon may come an urge to be a little more adventurous. If you have the space and the inclination, raising pigs – for breeding, for pork, for bacon, or all three – can be both rewarding and interesting. Pigs are social, intelligent and sensitive creatures, and contented pigs are quiet, happy animals.

For Caroline and Terry Alderton, the decision to raise two or three pigs each year came as a result of a desire to provide good quality pork, bacon and sausages for themselves, friends and family, but also to use up their regular stock of windfalls. This is an excellent food for pigs, and means they save on the cost of feeding them entirely on commercially-produced pig nuts. Caroline and Terry generally select rare breeds like Large Whites, Gloucester Old Spot or Large Blacks, as they believe these animals tend to be more placid and have a better flavour. They told me that they raise their pigs for love rather than profit, to provide themselves and others with meat from animals that have been well fed and cared for without the use of growth promoters.

FOOD, DRINK AND A FEW BITS MORE

Despite their reputation for being filthy animals, pigs manage their living quarters and themselves well, and should not result in a muddy or smelly display unless you fail in your animal husbandry. Yes, they like to forage in the soil and grass, but this is in search of nutrition in the form of vitamins, minerals, root vegetables and worms. And yes, they like to wallow in mud, but this is more for skin conditioning and to provide a sunscreen in hot weather. They never defecate or urinate in their own sleeping area and, even if left to their own devices, will organise separate areas of their living quarters for sleeping, eating and waste elimination. All you have to do is provide regular food and water, change their bedding and get rid of their waste (great fertiliser!).

Getting Started
Selection of breed depends partly on how you intend to rear the pigs and what you intend to do with their produce.

For rearing, the options are:

- Purchase young pigs or "weaners" at 6–8 weeks old weighing around 18 kg (40 lb) and raise them for six months to pork weight of 90–113 kg (200–250 lb) or 10 months to bacon weight.
- Purchase a sow "in pig" – a "gilt", a young female pig that is about to produce her first litter – then raise the offspring. A litter can be anything from 5–25 piglets; the average is 10–12.
- Keep a sow and boar and sell weaners.
- Keep a sow and boar and raise all offspring to pork or bacon weight.

There are numerous breeds to choose from; some of the most popular are:

Pork:	Berkshire, Landrace, Middle White
Bacon:	Large Black, Duroc
Dual-Purpose:	British Lop, Gloucester Old Spot, Saddleback, Tamworth

What You Need to Provide

Feed	Pig nuts (a grain-based feed). Feed should be provided twice per day. Pigs also like to eat fresh grass, forage for grubs, and root for swedes and turnips.

HOW TO LIVE ON LESS

Fresh water	All pigs need a constant supply of clean, fresh water to drink – between two and four gallons per day – but sows in milk need even more. Fix the water trough securely to the ground and make sure that the piglets can reach over the rim to drink the water.
Hose	Use a hose to top up the pigs' water holes or wallowing area.
Household scraps	Pigs will happily eat vegetable scraps and starchy food like cooked rice, pasta and potatoes (they should never be given meat).
Manual	Get yourself a really good manual on raising pigs.
Professional Support	Make sure you have foreknowledge of your local vet, abattoir, butcher and pig breeder, and keep an eye on the Defra website (www.defra.gov.uk) for pig-specific news and health alerts.
Secure outdoor area	Defra guidelines recommend no more than ten pigs per acre of land. You will also need either electric fencing, or secure post and rail fencing with pig netting, that can preferably be moved into different positions. Pigs will quickly exhaust supplies of grass and grubs, and effectively rotovate the area for you, eradicate weeds, plough and fertilise the soil, and demolish windfalls.
Shelter or ark	A basic hut made from simple materials such as iron or wood will enable a pig to shelter from sun and rain and house any piglets she may have.
Straw	Provide plenty of straw for the pigsty or shelter and change at least once a month.

Healthy Pigs

Always purchase your pigs from a registered pig breeder who will be able to provide you with the provenance of your pigs and the appropriate licences. Signs of good health include:

- a moist snout with bright eyes and general overall alertness
- a glossy, smooth hair coat, with the hairs lying close to the body

FOOD, DRINK AND A FEW BITS MORE

- a good appetite – a well-cared for young pig should put on 450–700 g (1-1½ lb) per day
- a curly tail – a straight tail may indicate illness
- a good underline (straight belly) with an evenly matched number of teats
- sociable with other pigs – one that is shunned by others may be unwell
- forward-pointing, not "ten to two" feet

Typical Daily Routine
Both Caroline and Terry have full-time jobs – their pig-raising activity is one of their living-on-less strategies – and the daily pig routine starts with a feed before work and a check that there are no signs of illness. They have an automatic drinking water dispenser that delivers water on demand, so the pigs have all they need for the day. On return from work, another feed is given and a second check is made. At the weekend, the pens are cleared out and the pen and fence checked over for necessary repairs. The weekend is also a time for Caroline and Terry to just enjoy being with their animals – the pigs love to have their backs and sides scratched and will readily collapse and roll over, inviting you to scratch their stomachs. They also love being hosed with water and playing with straw – they are "helping" to change their bedding – and also joining in a game of football. When it gets hot they just love to sunbathe – they can even get sunburnt if they don't put their sunscreen (mud) on!

Time to Break Even
Like chickens, you should always ensure you have a minimum of two pigs to keep each other company. If breeding, then you will need a sow and a boar.

I have made the following assumptions to simplify the Time to Break Even calculation:

- Purchase of two weaners: this is a minimum number to raise; increasing the number improves the Time to Break Even, particularly for follow-on years when infrastructure has already been purchased.
- Pigs are raised for six months to pork weight of 90–113 kg (200–250 lb).
- Usable meat (carcass weight) is 70 kg (154 lb).
- Pig ark suitable for housing two fully-grown porkers.
- Simple post and rail fencing with pig netting.
- Home-produced pork is sold at the same price as quality, organic, outdoor-reared commercial pork. This is pessimistic, as home-reared pork is likely to attract a premium price.

HOW TO LIVE ON LESS

Pigs with Infrastructure (Ark and Fencing)

Estimated cost of raising two pigs, including: • ark (£300) • post and rail fencing plus pig netting (£300) • two weaners (£80) • feed (£150) • slaughter (£40) • butcher (£60)	£930 (estimated)
Quantity of pork produced	70 kg (154 lb) carcass weight per pig times two pigs = 140 kg (308 lb)
Quantity of pork for own use	20 kg (1 joint or several chops per month)
Price of supermarket organic outdoor-reared pork	£8.65 per kg
Annual saving on purchase of pork	Quantity of pork times price of supermarket pork 20 x £8.65 = £173
Quantity of pork for sale	50 kg
Price of home-produced organic pork	£8.65 per kg
Revenue from home-produced pork	Quantity of pork for sale times price of home-produced pork 50 x £8.65 = £432.50
Total income and savings	Annual savings plus revenue £173 + £432.50 = £605.50
Time to Break Even	Cost of raising pigs divided by total income and savings £930 / £605.50 = 1 year 6 months

After the first year, once investment has been made in the initial cost of the ark and outdoor fencing, the Time to Break Even becomes more favourable.

FOOD, DRINK AND A FEW BITS MORE

Pigs without Infrastructure

Estimated cost of raising two pigs, including: • two weaners (£80) • feed (£150) • slaughter (£40) • butcher (£60)	£330 (estimated)
Quantity of pork produced	70 kg (154 lb) carcass weight per pig times two pigs = 140 kg (308 lb)
Quantity of pork for own use	20 kg (1 joint or several chops per month)
Price of supermarket organic pork	£8.65 per kg
Annual saving on purchase of pork	Quantity of pork times Price of supermarket pork 20 x £8.65 = £173
Quantity of pork for sale	50 kg
Price of home-produced organic pork	£8.65 per kg
Revenue from home-produced pork	Quantity of pork for sale times price of home-produced pork 50 x £8.65 = £432.50
Total income and savings	Annual savings plus revenue £173 + £432.50 = £605.50
Time to Break Even	Cost of raising pigs divided by total income and savings £330 / £605.50 = 6½ months

Using Produce from Pigs (Pork)

Pork Rillettes

Ingredients
900 g (2 lb) pork belly, rind removed and cut into short strips
300 g (10½ oz) lard
150 ml (¼ pint) wine
20 juniper berries, crushed
1½ tsp coarse salt
1½ tsp black pepper, ground
1 tbsp fresh thyme, leaves taken off the stalks
½ tsp each ground ginger, nutmeg, allspice and cloves
6 garlic cloves, peeled and cut into large chunks
3 fresh bay leaves

Method
1. Mix all the ingredients together and cook, covered, in a slow oven at 130ºC (250ºF) Gas $^1/_2$ for four hours.

2. Strain off the juices into a jug and refrigerate for half an hour to allow the fat to come to the surface. Take off the fat layer and return it to the pan – it will be used to cover the finished rillettes.

3. Shred the pork finely; mix with 5 tbsp juices from the jug and fill individual serving terrines, pressing down firmly.

4. Gently warm the pork fat until runny and pour a thin layer over the top of each terrine.

5. Allow to cool, then refrigerate overnight.

Thai Pork Salad
Don't stint on the herbs and spices in this recipe, otherwise the result will be too bland.

Ingredients
400 g (14 oz) lean pork, minced
2 tbsp water
2 tbsp fish sauce (nam pla)
2 tbsp lemon juice
1 onion, finely chopped
4 spring onions, finely chopped
2 tbsp peanuts or cashew nuts, roasted
2 tbsp ginger root, finely chopped
1 tbsp coriander leaf, finely chopped
4 tbsp mint leaf, finely chopped
$^1/_2$ chilli, finely chopped
1 lettuce, or other green salad vegetable to serve

Garnish
As well as garnishing with more nuts and fresh herbs – coriander, mint – try making some spring onion and/or chilli curls by slicing them lengthways, maintaining a 1 cm ($^1/_2$") stub intact, and placing in iced water to curl. Easy to achieve and looks authentically Thai.

FOOD, DRINK AND A FEW BITS MORE

Method
1. Put the pork and water into a pan and cook gently, stirring to ensure the pork mince stays crumbly rather than lumpy. If necessary, top up with water so that there is always about 3 tbsp in the pan.

2. Cool the pork for five minutes, then add the fish sauce, lemon juice, onions, spring onions, peanuts, ginger, coriander, mint and chilli. Toss gently to incorporate all the flavours.

3. Taste to see if any more fish sauce or lemon juice is needed. The mince can either be served immediately while still warm or left to cool completely – it's particularly refreshing if chilled in the fridge.

4. Serve on a bed of lettuce leaves and add your garnish.

Foraging

Reality Check: 🍸 ☺ (£-)

If you do just one thing: get down to the local hedgerow/forest/grassland and collect some wild food that you already recognise and know you will use – blackberries, cobnuts, dandelions.

Time to let out the hunter-gather in you! Foraging, or put more simply collecting food from the wild, takes us back to our primitive ancestors, who would have lived largely on the nuts, berries, fungi, greens, etc. that they were able to gather during the course of the day. It takes time and effort to forage for edibles but the rewards are very gratifying. You could have some unusual ingredients for the kitchen table, potentially also some excess for sale, gift or barter. And it represents food for free.

Foraging is perfectly legal, so long as what you are looking for – greens, berries, nuts, seeds, flowers, fruit, mushrooms – is growing wild, e.g. in woodland, grassland, hedgerow, etc., on land that you have a right to access (or have been given permission to access) and you are collecting for your own use.

As a child, my parents always took us brambling in September. I distinctly remember more blackberries going in my mouth than in the bag, but – hey! – that was really living! I remember the day as being a mix of excitement and trepidation. Where exactly are we going to look? What if we can't find any blackberries? Last year we found walnuts as well…will we this year? Last year we ate blackberry and apple pie/pudding/compote/whatever seemingly every day for a fortnight, and life was just great!

A few simple foraging rules:

- Take only enough for your own use – it might not cost you anything, but you do need to ensure that what gets left behind can recover and regenerate.
- Don't go foraging for fungi or wild greens unless you are confident you know what you are doing, or are accompanied by someone who does.
- Only take the parts of the plant – leaf, fruit – that are above ground, leaving the root system behind – it is in fact illegal to uproot even wild plants.
- Don't take any wild food that is damaged in any way.
- Always take one or more guidebooks to identify new species – you may know your greens very well, but what if you come across some interesting-looking fungi on the same trip?
- Preferably don't gather food from the roadside or anywhere where it may be contaminated with pollutants, chemical sprays or manure.
- Seek permission from landowners before foraging on private land.

Mushrooms

Far less casual than other foraging forays because of the need to make precise identification before you consume, mushrooming is nevertheless a rewarding experience and an effective mechanism for adding free food to your seasonal larder. The principal season is late summer and through the autumn, though a few species are available at other times of the year.

Mushrooms, or to be more precise fungi, are the fruiting bodies of an underground system of a white threadlike mass of filaments which form the vegetative part of the fungus known as *mycelium*. The mushrooms contain spores – a very useful aid in correct identification of the species – which are broadcast around the surrounding areas to reproduce and create more *mycelia*. It is therefore important that you only remove (by twisting, not cutting) the mushroom itself and not any of the underground root system.

There are something like 4,000 species of mushroom in the UK, but a large proportion of these are either poisonous or unpalatable. So you really

FOOD, DRINK AND A FEW BITS MORE

have to know what you are doing, and the best way is to join an experienced forager on a mushroom hunt. I guarantee you will enjoy your day. Just walking through woodland in the autumn is an absolute joy and a forager's paradise, or you might be taken across grassland or old pastures – and at the end of the day you will know how to look closely at the features of each mushroom so that you can then use a reference book to check whether it's edible or not. Once you are confident at identifying the signs of good mushroom habitats and are able to recognise and validate a small number of edible mushroom types, there is no reason why you shouldn't continue collecting alone, so long as you stick to what you know. I can't emphasise too strongly the need for caution when foraging for mushrooms. Safety is paramount, as eating an incorrectly identified mushroom could be fatal.

Once you know what you are doing, there are a few additional mushroom-collecting rules over and above the standard foraging rules given at the beginning of the section:

- Don't pick on a wet day and don't pick any mushroom that has any obvious signs of decay.
- Be absolutely sure of the identity of any mushrooms you plan to eat. If in doubt leave them.
- Only collect from a spot where there is already a good supply. Take no more than one-third of the population, and no more than 1.5 kg (3 lb 5 oz) across the whole foraging trip.
- Do not collect specimens that are too small.
- Place harvested mushrooms in a basket – they will decay very quickly if you put them into a plastic bag.
- Use within 24 hours of picking.

Drying Mushrooms
If you're not going to be eating mushrooms fresh, many wild mushrooms dry well.

1. Trim off any damaged parts.
2. Lay in a single layer on kitchen paper or on a tray in a warm, dry place for 12 hours or overnight to remove excess moisture.
3. Thread them onto strings like a long beaded necklace and hang them horizontally in the airing cupboard, or improvise over a radiator or an Aga, for several days.

4. Store when thoroughly dry and leathery in airtight boxes or wrapped in cling-film.
5. Reconstitute by soaking in warm water for about an hour before you use them – add the soaking liquid to the pot as well.

Note: the drying technique does not apply to cultivated mushrooms.

Cooking Mushrooms

Sautéed Mushrooms with Garlic and Parsley

My own preference for cooking and eating mushrooms is to keep it fairly simple: sauté the mushrooms with a little garlic in a frying pan into which you have melted in a fairly large knob of butter, with a little oil added to prevent burning. Wait until the mushrooms' juices start to flow, then pour the contents of the pan into a bowl and top with a large pinch of freshly chopped parsley – delicious! If you feel you need something to mop up all those lovely juices, either eat the mushrooms with a large hunk of crusty bread or pour them over some thickly cut toast.

Mushroom and Leek Soup

Ingredients
4 leeks, finely chopped
400 g (14 oz) mushrooms, finely chopped
Large pinch saffron stamens
600 ml (20 fl oz) vegetable stock
50 g (1¾ oz) butter
Salt and freshly ground black pepper
Grated nutmeg

Method
1. Gently heat the stock and add 2 tbsp to the saffron in a bowl; stir.

2. Melt butter in a saucepan and add the leeks and the mushrooms; cover and sweat for 10 minutes.

3. Add the stock, saffron, salt, pepper and a large pinch of nutmeg; simmer for 20 minutes.

FOOD, DRINK AND A FEW BITS MORE

Nuts, Fruit and Berries

When my husband was a child the local primary school encouraged children to gather rosehips – they were given 2d (old pence) per lb for their trouble, and he tells me he and his brother regularly harvested enough to earn themselves a shilling each. The school then made rose hip syrup – a hangover from wartime, I believe, when the Ministry of Food vaunted rose hip syrup to be a good substitute for orange juice. I don't think the financial inducement would be allowed now, but the principle is the same – collect from the countryside's free larder and produce something seasonal and nutritious for your family to consume.

Just up the road from where we live there are hedgerows a-plenty, and on a dry September day there are always a few people walking along, collecting whatever they can find. Apart from the opportunity to harvest some food for free, I like to go along for the pleasant walk and to pass the time of day with the fellow gatherers. Foragers have generally come from close by, know the lane well, and return each year. They have even divulged other "secret" venues where they forage for different crops – so now I also know where to head within walking distance to find elderberries, filberts and sloes. In my local lane you can be assured of a bumper crop of blackberries and crab apples, but we also gather dessert apples and damsons. I guess the latter two have grown in the wild from seeds dropped by birds, or even from cores and stones discarded by passing motorists (for which, I thank you!).

Just a brief word on nuts: you may find that some nuts you gather are somewhat smaller than the cultivated version and this makes them hard to crack and unlikely to end up in one piece. If you can put up with picking the shell out of the pulverised nut, then you'll be rewarded with a really tasty treat, suitable for making soups, pesto, adding to flapjack and crumble topping, or simply throwing over salads.

While pinecones are not going to feed your family, a walk through a pine forest late in the autumn will provide you with plenty of cones that you can use for your Christmas decorations. Mixed with holly, ivy, mistletoe and rosehips, all of which should also be around at his time of year, they can form a very pleasant display, either arranged in a willow basket or fixed to a circular frame to create a wreath.

HOW TO LIVE ON LESS

Using Nuts, Fruit and Berries

Nut Soup
Ingredients
50 g (1¾ oz) nuts – almonds, hazelnuts, walnuts, cobnuts – whatever you can find
1 tbsp chopped parsley
1 medium potato, chopped
1 carrot, chopped
1 small onion, chopped
1 garlic clove, finely chopped
2 tsp honey
1 litre (1¾ pints) stock

Method
1. Pour a little water into a saucepan, bring to the boil and then "water-fry" the onion, garlic, carrot and potato on a gentle heat.

2. Liquidise the nuts with about one-third of the stock – the smoother the resultant paste, the better.

3. Add the cooked vegetables to the nut paste and liquidise with a little more stock.

4. Pour into a saucepan with the remaining stock, honey and parsley and simmer for 15–20 minutes.

5. Check the seasoning and add salt and pepper if required.

6. Ladle into warm bowls, sprinkle with parsley and serve.

Crab Apple Jelly
Ingredients
1.8 kg (4 lb) crab apples
1.2 litres (2 pints) water
1.8–2.25 kg (4–5 lb) sugar

Sugar thermometer (optional)

Method
1. Wash the apples, taking out any damaged pieces, then cut into even-sized chunks – no need to peel or core.

2. Bring the water to the boil in a large saucepan, then add the apples; simmer until fruit is soft and pulpy.

3. Sieve the pulp into a large bowl – this will probably take several hours – but don't be tempted to force it through.

4. Measure the liquid. For each 250 ml (9 fl oz) of juice add 250 g (9 oz) of sugar.

5. Dissolve gently over heat, then bring to the boil.

6. Continue to boil for 10–15 minutes or until the sugar thermometer reads 104°C (220°F). If you don't have a sugar thermometer, put a teaspoon of the jam in a saucer in the freezer for a few minutes. If you cannot make a clean line through the jam with your finger, continue to boil; if it holds itself apart and wrinkles round the edges, then it's ready.

7. Remove from the heat. Pour into warmed, sterilised jars, cover, seal and label when cold.

Variations
Add chopped herbs – mint is especially good to make a mint jelly – both at step 2 to add flavour and at step 4 to add visible pieces of herbs. Experiment with different herbs and with different quantities at each stage depending on your taste.

Add 1 tsp cinnamon or large pinch ground cloves at the beginning.

Wild Greens

> ⓘ Did you know…? Dandelion florets have a similar, if less pungent, quality to saffron? Create a little "tea bag" by wrapping the florets in muslin tied with a long piece of string to dangle over the edge of the pan, then drop into savoury rice dishes (paella, risotto, pilao) as they cook or into the hot milk infusion before making milk puddings (crème brulée, custard, rice pudding, etc.).

HOW TO LIVE ON LESS

Edible greens can be found almost all year round and in all sorts of places, from woodland to hedgerows, and on marshy ground. Take a walk in any of these areas and you'll discover a vast wild larder that you can harvest for free.

Like anything you find in the wild, you do need to be sure of what you are harvesting. I guess most of us can recognise stinging nettles (and there's a sure but painful mechanism of finding out whether you're right!), but unless you are familiar with some of the other wild greens that are common and good to eat – see table below – then make sure you have a good book that gives clear pictures and a detailed description. If you have collected something edible that you've never tried before, only eat a small amount first as, like anything, it may disagree with you. Also, wild greens generally have a more pronounced bitter taste than we are used to from cultivated crops – so, again, harvest in small quantities until you know what you like and how much you will need for your own use.

Wild greens have at least as much flavour and nutrition as do the cultivated varieties and – best of all – don't need to be sown, watered…or even weeded.

Wild Greens	Information
Alexanders *Smyrnium olustratum* (aka Hedge Parsley)	Mainly coastal plant; very early blooming along hedgerows and on sheltered slopes leading down to the shore. Has a strong celery-like flavour. Eat raw in salads or cooked in soups and stews. Leafy seedlings can be used as a parsley substitute; spicy seeds are used as a pepper substitute. Robust umbrella-shaped, greenish-yellow flower heads.
Chickweed *Stellaria media*	Available all year round if the winter is not too severe. Flavour similar to cress. Highly nutritious, chickweed can be added to salads; the cooked leaves are barely distinguishable from spring spinach. Seed can be ground into a powder and used in making bread or to thicken soups; the leaves are very small to be picked off individually, so strip them off the stem with a fork; use the stem as well.

FOOD, DRINK AND A FEW BITS MORE

Common nettle *Urtica dioica* (aka stinging nettle)	This "weed" absorbs every substance it can from the soil and passes it on to the consumer. It is therefore a very nutritious food that is easily digested and is high in minerals (especially iron) and vitamins (especially A and C). Collect leaf from March to November from wasteland, hedgerow, ditches, grassland. Young leaves can be cooked as a pot herb and added to soups. Cooking the leaves, or thoroughly drying them, neutralizes the sting, rendering the leaf safe to eat. Also makes a good tisane, and can be added to the beer-making process. An excellent compost accelerator.
Common sorrel *Rumex acetosa*	These are among the first green shoots for spring. The plant looks like a small dock with pointed, spear-shaped leaves. Delicious lemony flavour which can overpower other flavours, so use as a salad contributor rather than on its own. A drink similar to lemonade (but without the fizz) can be made by boiling up the leaves.
Dandelion *Taraxacum officinale*	The "crowns" or rosettes should be gathered when the leaves are very young and tender, before the flower has formed; the plant is less bitter in winter. Chicory-like flavour. Rich in Vitamin A and potassium. Use as an addition to herbal beer (especially with burdock); two-year-old root makes a decent coffee substitute; the flowers can be made into wine; the florets are a decent saffron substitute.
Fat Hen *Chenopodium album*	Fleshy stems, angular leaves. Spinach substitute, but should be cooked; the seed can be sprouted to add to salads.

Good Kind Henry *Chenopodium bonus-henricus*	Similar to Fat Hen. Triangular leaves. Rich in vitamin C, calcium and thiamine. Take quickly from harvest to pot, then use as a pot herb or a spinach substitute; fry the flowers in butter.
Hop *Humulus lupulus*	The female flowers provide the characteristic bitter taste in beer. The tips of young shoots are edible - add to salads or cook like asparagus. The flowers are soporific - make into a hop pillow to help you sleep.
Jack-by-the-hedge *Alliara petiolata* (aka garlic mustard)	Late spring. Fresh-looking, broad, pale-green leaves stand out in woodland shade. A brassica (part of the cabbage family) which can be finely chopped and added to a salad; used to be used in cooking to flavour fish and meat.
Wood sorrel *Oxalis acetosella*	Three leaflets, five-petal white or lilac flowers; at night or in wet weather the leaflets fold together. Delicious lemony flavour; oxalic acid and has a scouring quality, so people with gastric inflammation or kidney stones shouldn't eat much if at all.
Cleavers *Galium aparine*	March. The seeds can be ground up and roasted for coffee; eat the young fresh leaves in salads.

Using Wild Greens

If you find the bitterness of wild greens a little overpowering for your taste, especially for a salad, try soaking them first in cold water with a little coarse salt added for 30 minutes.

To start with, you might find it best to add a few wild greens to tried-and-tested recipes like vegetable stir-fries or leafy soups, until you are confident you are happy with the flavour.

FOOD, DRINK AND A FEW BITS MORE

Wild Greens Soup

Ingredients
2 potatoes, peeled and chopped
2 shallots, peeled and chopped
2 celery sticks, chopped
1 clove garlic, finely chopped
450 g wild greens – either one variety or selection of several – leaves separated from stalk
1 litre vegetable stock
Coarse salt and ground black pepper to taste

Method
1. Cook the potatoes until tender; drain.

2. Put 2 tbsp water into a saucepan and "water fry" the shallots, celery and garlic until soft.

3. Add the stock, potatoes and wild greens and simmer for ten minutes.

4. Cool slightly, then liquidise and return to the pan through a sieve. Adjust the seasoning if necessary.

5. Warm through to serving temperature.

Road Kill

If, like me, you're the sort of person that reads the end of the book first, then your particular reward (punishment?) is that you get to read the one aspect of living on less that is really not my cup of tea – road kill.

Road kill means taking those creatures that have had the misfortune to have been killed on the road – rabbits, ducks, pheasants, pigeons, squirrels, badger, deer – and using them to supplement your own larder. Actually, though the whole subject of road kill frankly appals me, it's a completely ethical exercise, and I can see its value in providing free food for you as well as your pets. I also think eating road kill has got to be a lot healthier and more nutritious (assuming you have collected good, fresh meat) than eating just about any kind of junk food.

HOW TO LIVE ON LESS

Anyway, it's entirely up to you whether you pursue this type of foraging for yourself. If you do, there are a few rules you need to know:

1. You may not remove animals that you have hit or run over yourself.
2. Only collect road kill that you know is fresh – for example, if you travel the same road morning and evening and the kill wasn't there on the last journey, you can assume it's sufficiently fresh.
3. Never collect anything that is puffy, flat or has been splattered.

Of course, having found a suitable mechanism for getting your road kill back home without it staining the inside of your car or your jacket, you will then have to skin, bone and eviscerate the animal yourself and discard the parts you aren't going to eat.

INDEX

Index

Air miles	63	Days out	64
Arts and crafts	83	Deterrents and barriers,	
Auctions	17, 25	natural	128
		Direct debit	21, 28
Beekeeping	150–159	Discount vouchers	19, 24
Beer, home-brewed	134–139	Dishwasher	49
Berries	179–181	Drinks, non-alcoholic	146
Beverages	134	Duty-free outlets	24
Bio-fuel	55		
Bio-mass	54	Electricity	27
Boiler efficiency	41	generating	30
Books	66	micro-generation systems	30
Brandy	145	sell-back (to the grid)	34, 36
Budgeting	13	Energy saving	45
Business networks	18	e-trading	17
		Everyday consumables	86
Cash	20		
Cashback portals	17	Fitness	65
Cashflow	14	Foraging	175
Charity shops	22	Freecycle	18
Chickens	159–168	Fruit	109–115, 179–181
Cleaning products, natural	70–73	Fuel	53
Clothes	66		
Community networks	18, 65	Garden	49, 90
Compact fluorescent lamps		Grants	31, 36, 38, 42, 44, 58
(CFLs)	45	Ground source heat pumps	44
Companion planting	127		
Comparison websites	19, 28, 48, 60	Heating	38
		generating heat	42
Compost	131	reducing heat loss	39
Computers	67	Herbal recipes	122, 123
Cooking	88	Herb garden	116
Cosmetics, natural	75–81	harvesting and preserving	119
Credit	20	planting plan	117
Credit card	20	Herbs	115, 120
Crop rotation plan	96	Holidays	63
Cut flower garden	123	Home	59

HOW TO LIVE ON LESS

Income	14	Radiators	58
Insulation	39	Rainwater	51
Integral back boiler	58	storing and reusing	52
Internet	16, 67	Reduce - reuse - recycle	73
		Road kill	185
Leftover food	74		
Lighting	45	Salads	92, 94
light-emitting diodes		Self-sufficiency	26, 91
(LEDs)	47	Shops	22
Liquid petroleum gas (LPG)	54	Shopping	86
Livestock	149	revolution	11
Local exchange trading		Skype	67
schemes (LETS)	18	Sloe gin	146
Loyalty schemes	23	Smoothies	147
		Social networks	18
Micro-greens	93	Solar energy	30
Micro-hydro	37	Solar garden lights	47
Multi-purchase deals	23	Solar thermal systems	42
Mushrooms	176–178		
Music	66	Tax-free outlets	24
		Thermostat level	40
Nuts	179–181	Toilet flush	48
		Travel	61, 62
Online shopping	16, 64		
Own brand	23	Underfloor heating	58
Outgoings	14	Unwanted goods	75
Outlets	22		
Out-of-town superstores	22	Vegetable garden	105
		using produce from	105–109
Packaging	73	Vegetable patch	95
Personal wash	49	Vegetables	92
Pest controls			
(indoors), natural	82, 83		
(outdoors), natural	126		
Photovoltaic (pv) cells	31		
Pigs	168–175		
Planning	15		
Planning permission	33, 37		
Preparing food	49		

INDEX

Washing machine	49
Water	48
reusing domestic	51
Wax	157
Wild greens	181–185
Wildlife	129
Wind turbines	34
Wines	139–144
Wood-burning stove	56
Wood chips	57
Wood fuel briquettes	58
Wood pellets	57

ALSO AVAILABLE FROM W & H PUBLISHING

How to Start and Run Your Own Home-based Business

AUTHOR: Matthew Thomas,
ISBN: 978-0-9561091-0-1
PRICE: £12.99
PAGES: 240
FORMAT: 234 mm x 155 mm
COVER: Full colour
BINDING: Paperback

How to Start and Run Your Own Home-based Business is the new book for budding entrepreneurs by writer, consultant and home-business expert Matthew Thomas.

The book takes you through everything you need to consider before starting a home-based business – from assessing the pros and cons, through drawing up a business plan and cashflow forecast, to matters such as marketing and credit control, and later deciding when and how to expand. The book is crammed with detailed practical advice, backed up by carefully researched facts, figures and contact information.

For anyone hoping to join the 2.1 million people currently running a home-based business in the UK, it's essential reading.

W & H Publishing, Apple Tree Cottage, Inlands Road, Nutbourne, Chichester, West Sussex, PO18 8RJ. Tel.: 01243 375006, E-mail: jon@lotuspublishing.co.uk
Distribution: *Combined Book Services*, Unit Y, Paddock Wood Distribution Centre, Paddock Wood, Tonbridge, Kent, TN12 6UU. Tel.: 01892 837171; Fax.: 01892 837272.